From Partition to Progress

From Partition to Progress

Persecuted Hindus and the Struggle for Citizenship

Anirban Ganguly

ISBN: 978-93-6547-828-0

First published in India 2024
This edition published 2024

BluOne Ink Pvt. Ltd
A-76, 2nd Floor, Sector 136, Noida
Uttar Pradesh 201301
www.bluone.ink
publisher@bluone.ink

Kali, Occam and BluPrint are all trademarks of BluOne Ink Pvt. Ltd.

Contents

To
Dr Syama Prasad Mookerjee (1901–1953)
Staunchest friend and leader of Bengali Hindus during
their darkest hours in history

Prefatory Thoughts

Until the election of a decisive, performance-oriented and focused government led by Prime Minister Narendra Modi, Indian politics and governance were suffering from the deadly disease of the vote bank. Issues of national interest, cultural identity, civilizational causes, and humanitarian and governance concerns were mostly decided taking into account the considerations and compulsions of the vote bank. It was, thus, not surprising to see that when the moment came to correct the injustices done to victims of the Radcliffe line which had demarcated a partitioned India in 1947 and had inflicted untold miseries on a large number of people, some political parties—especially those who have ruled India for the longest period of time—prioritized their positions in Parliament driven by considerations of the vote bank.

It was ironic to see them opposing the Citizenship Amendment Act (CAA), more so because many leaders of these parties in the past had at times argued in favour of rehabilitating and conferring citizenship rights on minorities from Pakistan and Bangladesh. Shifting goalposts, these parties and their leaders went all out in opposing the passing of the Citizenship Amendment Bill, 2019. The parties which have most indulged in vote-bank politics and rule border states like West Bengal most raucously opposed the passage of the Bill that spoke of conferring citizenship to a large number of beleaguered minorities from India's neighbourhood.

The Congress party, which was responsible for the partition of the country and is the originator of infiltration and demography-related problems of Assam, opposed the Bill in the House giving a message that India does not really belong to persecuted Hindus and Sikhs. The Trinamool Congress (TMC), which spoke out in support of Rohingya infiltrators and opposed the Government of India's move to identify Rohingya infiltrators and deport them and whose leader Mamata Banerjee was seen to speak in support of West Bengal providing shelters to Rohingyas, opposed the Bill simply because those who benefitted from this were Hindus, Sikhs, Jains, Christians, and Parsis. They seemed to have no consideration or sympathy for these minorities in our neighbouring countries. They did not seem to be concerned with their human rights. It was as if they didn't even deserve to be recognized as persecuted and therefore entitled to Indian citizenship. It was unfortunate to see Congress oppose the Bill tooth and nail.

Congress leader Rahul Gandhi pledged to oppose CAA 'tooth and nail'. As this opuscule will show, Rahul Gandhi's great-grandfather had consistently opposed the granting of citizenship rights to persecuted minorities from India's neighbourhood. Nehru was especially opposed to and acerbic towards the Bengali Hindu refugees. It is known that the Congress, as a party, has always betrayed the Hindus of Pakistan and East Pakistan and later Bangladesh. It failed to keep its promise to protect them.

Some leaders of the Left parties had in the past expressed their support for citizenship for refugees from Pakistan, but they turned out to be hypocrites on the floor of the House by opposing CAA, which would have provided them with that citizenship. It also revealed the truth that the Congress, communist parties, and the TMC have only used the refugees to further their political agenda and have never attempted to give them a dignified existence and permanent citizenship in this country.

It is pertinent to mention that the majority of these refugees belong to the Schedule Castes. However, the Bahujan Samaj Party (BSP) and Ms Mayawati, who claim to be the messiah of Harijans in India, could not gather the courage to support the Bill fearing that this would antagonize their Muslim votebank. The propaganda that the CAA violated Article 14, compromised the secular character of the Constitution and was anti-Muslim needed to be clarified to expose the hypocrisy and double standard of India's political opposition. Union Home Minister Amit Shah has clarified—not once but a number of times—on the floor of both Houses of Parliament while debating the CAA, that it had nothing to do with Indian Muslims and that Muslims who are Indian citizens need not be worried on account of the passage of the Bill, that the Bill is not meant to take away anyone's citizenship but is meant to confer citizenship.

Interestingly, if one were to look into the past, many prominent members of the Constituent Assembly like Pt Thakurdas Bhargava, Sardar Bhopinder Singh Man, and Professor Shibbanlal Saxena raised their voices on 11 and 12 August 1949 for giving citizenship to Hindus and Sikhs across the globe who consider India as their only homeland.

Pt Jawaharlal Nehru vetoed the idea. Sardar Bhopinder Singh Man had argued,

> They are as much sons of the soil as anyone else. This political mishap was not of their own seeking and now it will be very cruel to place these political impediments in their way and debar them from coming over to Bharat Mata. Our demand is that any person, who because of communal riots in Pakistan has come over to India and stayed here at the commencement of this Constitution, should automatically be considered as a citizen of India and should on no account be made to go to a registering authority and plead before him and establish a qualification of six months domicile to claim rights of citizenship.

Pandit Thakur Das Bhargava's words in the Constituent Assembly are strikingly relevant in the context of the CAA debate:

> I am desirous that not a single person who has come from Pakistan as a refugee should have any trouble in being a citizen of India. I am anxious that no obstacle should be placed in the way of those refugees who have come from Pakistan on account of disturbances and who have left their hearths and homes and come to this country.

In the case of Pakistan's failure to ensure the rights of its minorities, they become the responsibility of the Indian state and cannot be left to die or be faced with forced conversion. This was an unfinished agenda of India's partition. The NDA-I government, led by Atal Bihari Vajpayee as prime minister, had conferred special rights to district collectors in Rajasthan and Gujarat to decide the applications for citizenship for Hindu and Sikh refugees. Prime Minister Narendra Modi's historic commitment and promise made in 2014 and again in 2019, to pass the Bill and grant citizenship has now been fulfilled. When he promised to pass the CAA, he was fulfilling a commitment that began with the Bharatiya Jana Sangh (BJS) decades ago and was kept alive by the Bharatiya Janata Party (BJP), without break, for decades. In this context let us recall how the Congress by opposing the CAA has even forsaken its leaders and former Prime Minister. Dr Manmohan Singh, Leader of Opposition in the Rajya Sabha, while speaking on the Citizenship Amendment Bill 2003, urged the then Deputy Prime Minister and Home Minister of India L.K. Advani to take note of the plight of the refugees:

> I would like to say something about the treatment of refugees. After the partition of our country, the minorities in countries like Bangladesh have faced persecution, and it is our moral obligation that if circumstances force people, these unfortunate people, to seek refuge in our country, our approach to granting citizenship to these unfortunate persons should be more liberal. I sincerely hope that the Honorable Deputy Prime Minister will bear this in mind in charting out the future course of action with regard to the Citizenship Act.

Participating in the discussion, former chief of the Indian Army General Shankar Roy Chowdhury, then a member of the Rajya Sabha from West Bengal, spoke of the refugees and illegal migrants and called for conferring citizenship to them. He said,

It is an issue I had taken up with the hon. Deputy Prime Minister. From Bangladesh, we are getting a wide variety of people who are entering into our country illegally, all of them. Some are economic migrants whom you see all over the country, be it Mumbai, Delhi or Calcutta. Some are infiltrators, terrorists. But a large number of them are religious minorities facing persecution, Chakmas, Hindus, Buddhists, many of them. I urge the Government again, through you, Madam—I earnestly urge the Government— minorities fleeing Bangladesh for the fear of persecution should be given citizenship and should be treated in a supportive and kind manner.

Shankar Roy Chowdhury was an all-party-supported candidate for the Rajya Sabha from West Bengal and had a distinguished record of leading the armed forces. Did the parties that nominated him agree to his demand in 2003? They vocally opposed the CAA in 2019.

On the objection that CAA discriminates against Muslims, it must be understood that it offers a future and a protected existence for minorities who are facing religious persecution in Pakistan, Afghanistan, and Bangladesh. Since these three countries—Pakistan, Afghanistan, and Bangladesh are declared Islamic republics—and since Muslims are neither oppressed nor are they minorities there, they are not eligible for Indian citizenship.

This classification in the CAA qualifies the test of 'Reasonable Classification' for giving preferential treatment as has been laid down for Article 14 and is in consonance with the law of the land. There is no religious discrimination in the CAA. It ascertains the interests of the minorities and, as per the commitment given to them during Partition, focuses on fulfilling that commitment. The opposition parties stand exposed as they have fumbled on their commitment to these refugees and are blinded by vote-bank politics.

Dr Syama Prasad Mookerjee resigned from the Nehru Cabinet in opposition to the Nehru–Liaqat Pact inked on 8 April 1950. He foresaw that the 'Delhi Agreement' would fail. It was unfortunate that in order to pander to a pseudo-secular mindset, millions of refugees, who were the victims of religious persecution in Pakistan were sacrificed. Dr Mookerjee's words still ring true in the context of the CAA debate:

> Let us not forget that the Hindus of East Bengal are entitled to the protection of India, not on humanitarian considerations alone, but by virtue of their sufferings and sacrifices, made cheerfully for generations, not for advancing their own parochial interest, but for laying the foundations of India's political freedom and intellectual progress. It is the united voice of the leaders that are dead and of the youth that smilingly walked up to the gallows for India's cause that calls for justice and fair-play at the hands of Free India of today.

While he tabled the Citizenship Amendment Bill, 2019, in the Lok Sabha, Union Home Minister Amit Shah asked a fundamental question when he was responding to Adhir Ranjan Chowdhury, the Congress party's leader in the House. The latter, because he comes from infiltrator-dominated Murshidabad, was repeatedly obstructing the placing of the Bill. Shah asked why the Bill had to be tabled. It had to be, he answered, because in 1947, the Congress had partitioned this country on the basis of religion. This is the stark truth that needs to be told, that this Bill and this herculean effort that is going into remedying this historic wrong, is because the Congress party had capitulated before Jinnah's communal blackmail.

The BJS and BJP have never overlooked this dimension of our Partition history. Right since their inception, they had continuously advocated the cause of the Hindus of either part of Pakistan and had demanded that the Indian leadership fulfil its promised duties towards these minorities in the neighbourhood. During the historic campaigns in 2014 and 2019, Prime Minister Narendra Modi has repeatedly referred to this historic commitment and promised to bring it into effect.

Ever since, the Congress party, during Nehru's era and later, has been lukewarm to the plight of the Bengali Hindu refugees and to the fact that Hindus were being forced to come away from Pakistan and Bangladesh. Nehru refused to heed Dr Syama Prasad Mookerjee's repeated exhortation that there be a complete exchange of population on the eastern front as well and kept harping on his demand that the Bengali Hindu refugee must go back to East Bengal. Speaking in Parliament on 7 August 1950, Dr Mookerjee made a historic intervention in the 'Bengal situation'. Among the many forceful and reasonable points he made, Dr Mookerjee reiterated his call for a complete exchange of population, property plus compensation, in the eastern region:

> Our Prime Minister says that it goes against his faith. He kept his faith in cold storage while India was partitioned. He kept his faith in cold storage when he had himself to

organise exchange in the Punjab. He organised special trains to take Muslims to the other side – maybe not individually but his Government…. He realised what was happening, namely, that Hindus and Sikhs were coming out and Muslims were going away and so he thought: 'Let us make it possible for them to go away.' I feel that here also, at another time, he has to put his faith in cold storage.

The foundation of the Nehru–Liaquat Pact of April 1950 was meant to facilitate that false hope. While a large number of Muslims who had gone to East Pakistan had returned to West Bengal, the Hindus who went back to East Pakistan could not survive. They were hounded and driven out to return to West Bengal and had to eke out an existence as refugees without elementary dignity and a source of livelihood.

As Dr Mookerjee asked during his historic intervention in Parliament on 7 August 1950, when the House discussed in detail the 'Bengal Situation': 'What was the main purpose of the Pact [Nehru–Liaquat Pact]?' He asked the House,

Was not the chief object of the pact that Hindus would be able to live in East Bengal with a sense of security and without fear; that there would be no exodus and those who had come away would gradually of their own accord feel emboldened to go back to their home? Was it not the purpose of the Pact that there would be a sense of security in the minds of the minorities [in East Pakistan/Bengal] themselves so that they could decide on their own course of action without any fear or expectation of favour from any quarter? Judged from this standpoint the Pact has failed.

The main test of the pact, Dr Mookerjee had argued, 'would be whether conditions of security are being created in East Bengal whereby Hindus can live there out of their own free will'. It was evident within weeks of the pact being inked that it had failed. Dr Mookerjee, basing himself on data from the ground, his people having carried out extensive surveys, clinically proved how the Pact was indeed a non-starter as far as Hindus of East Bengal were concerned:

> Beginning from 14th June 1950 and ending on 3rd August 1950 … 15,900 Hindus had been interrogated by our workers. Out of these 15,900 Hindus who were going back to East Bengal about 90 per cent of them declared that they had no intention whatsoever to go and stay in East Bengal. About 10 per cent said they wanted to make an attempt to live in East Bengal. But even amongst that ten per cent, there was a good percentage of people who said that they did not wish to go back to East Bengal but that they found conditions of refugees and living in West Bengal to be so hard and oppressive that they had no option but to go back and make another trial. In the same way I had advised my workers to interrogate the Muslims who were going to East Bengal. Of course, not all Muslims were willing to answer the interrogation for obvious reasons. We could get an answer from 4,500 Muslims and their answer was that about 40 per cent of them were going away to live in East Bengal but 60 per cent wanted to come back to West Bengal…. Now, what does these statistics show? That in the mind of 90 per cent of the Hindus who were going back to East Bengal there is no return of confidence at all. On the other hand, in the minds of the Muslims, 60 per cent of them feel confident to live in West Bengal and India.

Dr Mookerjee then listed out the atrocities committed on the Hindus in East Bengal after the Pact. A stunned House along with the prime minister listened with rapt attention while he said,

> So far as the incidents which have happened in East Bengal after the Pact, I have got a summary of them between 8th April and 30th of June 1950.... The incidents about which we have got the written evidence of individuals who have suffered. I shall only read a summary of this list. Between the date of the pact and 30th June 1950, there have been 757 cases of dacoity, robbery and theft, 219 cases of extortion, 194 cases of trespass, 180 cases of assault, harassment and threats to leave Pakistan, 129 cases of abduction, rape and outraging the modesty of females, 70 cases of murder, 70 cases of grievous hurt, stabbing and looting, 67 cases of arson, 21 cases of wrongful confinement and restraint, 39 cases of defiling Hindu temples and places of worship and 72 cases of illegal possession.... By no means is this an exhaustive list. This is only an illustrative list of occurrences which have happened in East Bengal right up to 30th June 1950, and spread almost throughout the length and breadth of Eastern Bengal. In every one of these cases, I should add the minority, the Hindus is the victim and the oppressor is a member of the majority community. The entire social and economic structure in which Hindus lived has collapsed and it is impossible for them to live there.

Dr Mookerjee also cited specific examples. His information was thorough, and his sources were impeccable. He was careful not to base himself on surmise or hearsay:

> This is a typical case. Here was a family who after the Pact wanted to go back to Barisal and they did go back. Within a

week of their return, their house was attacked. The father, an
old man, who was a retired Police Sub-Inspector was killed.
The mother was seriously stabbed and the son also, but both
escaped death, miraculously. The mother and the son came
away to Calcutta; they came to me and we did arrange for
their medical treatment through Government agency. This
is the story which the son gave and I presented the son in
person to some Members of the House, so that those hon.
Members of the House could satisfy themselves that these
were not concocted stories as Pakistan Government usually
says.

Dr Mookerjee told the House that during his visit to
Agartala in the state of Tripura, officers who met him
on the day he arrived were anxious since they had
been receiving telegram messages that 'some families
which they had persuaded to go back to East Bengal
from Agartala' had gone back and 'some of them were
butchered', while 'others who were still clinging to their
villages were forced to come away'. He spoke of school
teachers who had attempted to go back to East Bengal
after the Pact. They had to come back, and they narrated
their torturous experience. Dr Mookerjee told the House
and Prime Minister Nehru,

> It breaks my heart to say this, but it is as well that the Prime
> Minister and the House should know that this is the state
> to which the Hindus in East Bengal have been reduced.
> Demands are often made of their womenfolk at night, that
> they ought to go to a Muslim's house at night and return
> home next morning. There are people who are submitting
> to this ignominy because they find themselves unable to
> counteract this aggression. This is what is happening.

He appealed to Nehru that he 'should himself go down to Calcutta and live with the refugees' and that he should not 'depend upon his paper statistics', should throw them into the waste-paper basket, and 'stand before the human statistics there'. He told the prime minister how these refugees had told him, and begged him to ask 'Sardar Patel and Panditji, "Have they forgotten us? Let them come and stay with us, we shall tell them how we have suffered, let them share with us our sorrows, our humiliations and our miseries".... This is what the people are expecting the Prime Minister to do'. Dr Mookerjee accused Nehru of avoiding the refugees from East Bengal, of not trying to understand their pitiable conditions and of making sweeping statements regarding how the Pact was working:

> He [Nehru] went to Calcutta a few weeks ago and the only public function which he could find time to attend was the dinner given by the Muslims where he was hailed as 'Shahansha'. Psychologically he committed a grievous mistake. If for five minutes – I know his magnetic personality – he had gone and stayed with these sufferers, I know his heart would have melted. Stones melt, I have no doubt Jawaharlal's heart would have melted. Let him not take these facts from me, from his officers. I would ask him to go straight to the individuals, stay with them, enter into their hearts and understand their suffering. Then only he will be able to tackle the problem. There is no use playing with figures. Whom does he satisfy by saying that there is a return to normalcy because five lakhs of people are going back to stay in East Bengal? Five lakhs are not going to stay there. I have got it on the authority of the people who are still there. India must make up her mind.

Dr Mookerjee tabled a resolution which the Hindus of Mymensingh in East Bengal had passed in a Convention they held on 13 June 1950.

He handed a copy to the prime minister and said, 'What do they say? They say that conditions are in existence which if not changed will make it extremely difficult for any Hindu to live there.' He cited a particular paragraph of this historic resolution which said that the Convention:

> regrets to note that in spite of the Nehru-Liaquat Agreement to rehabilitate the returned migrants in their original homes, most of the migrants, on return, are getting no help from authorities and are living in pitiable, deplorable conditions, without any shelter, without any means of subsistence. Their own houses are under occupation of Muslim refugees from India and the arable lands of these evacuees have been distributed to them. The efforts of the Members of the District Minority Boards and the Minority Commission have so far been fruitless, and the indifferent attitude of Government is causing immense hardship to the returned people.

Dr Mookerjee spoke of the:

> fellow-workers of the great leaders who adorn the Treasury Benches [of the Indian Parliament] today. They mention their names and ask, 'Have they forgotten us? Do they not think of us? Who gave them freedom? They are today occupying positions of power and authority in Delhi. Who made them what they are? Do they remember that we also contributed to the freedom of the country and gave whatever we had without expecting anything in return? And today when we are in this [troublesome] state, when we are being hounded out like cats and dogs, without getting

any protection which any civilised Government worth the name is bound to give are they not thinking of us?'

Obviously, the pact had failed. In his historic statement in Parliament upon his resignation, Dr Mookerjee reminded those who had questioned the need for India to fulfil its promise:

> Let us not forget that the Hindus of East Bengal are entitled to the protection of India, not on humanitarian considerations alone, but by virtue of their sufferings and sacrifices, made cheerfully for generations, not for advancing their own parochial interests, but for laying the foundations of India's political freedom and intellectual progress. It is the united voices of leaders that are dead and of the youth that smilingly walked up to the gallows for India's cause that calls for justice and fair-play at the hands of Free India of today.

Forty years into exile in the French enclave of Pondicherry, not active in politics any longer, Sri Aurobindo had the sage's foresight to see how the Nehru–Liaquat Pact was a clever ruse by Liaquat Ali Khan to save Pakistan. To a disciple who wanted to know his views on the Pact, Sri Aurobindo wrote that he regarded the 'pact as an exceedingly clever move of Liaquat Ali to fish his "nation" out of the desperate situation into which it had run itself and to secure its safe survival'. Nehru could not see what most could perceive.

The *Amrita Bazar Patrika*'s editorial of 26 May 1950 starkly argued,

> [That the] success of the Delhi Agreement depends, not on radio talks or ministerial tours, not even on well-considered

administrative measures, but on the establishment of 'real friendship', between the two States. That 'real friendship' cannot be established so long as the Kashmir issue is not settled 'justly'. The Hindus of East Bengal must, therefore, remain victims of caprice: today the Agreement may bring them some relief, tomorrow communal frenzy may put them in hell. Bluntly speaking, they are hostages for India's conduct in Kashmir.

But Nehru, in his ostrich-like attitude and driven by an overbearing sense of false prestige, was prepared to put at stake the lives of minorities in East Bengal.

It was this failure of the Pact that added to the woe of the Bengali Hindu refugees who became rootless and felt abandoned. Dr Mookerjee's intervention during this debate in free India's provisional parliament is also deeply disturbing—both because, having extensively travelled across the area where the refugees had come to seek shelter and having interacted with them, he gave an authentic and heart-rending description of their status and the challenges and persecutions that compelled them to leave their home and hearth. Speaking of the failure of the Nehru–Liaquat Pact, Dr Mookerjee argued that it was impossible for the Hindus to continue to survive in East Bengal because the 'loot mentality has been roused. The blood lust is there. The lust to abduct women is there. You cannot escape from the telling and terrible facts.' He reminded the Mahatma's disciples in the House that a few weeks before his death, during a prayer meeting, Gandhi had said that if 'minorities in Eastern Bengal are not protected, let the Government of India take action'. Among the many points, suggestions and cautions that he made during this prescient intervention,

Dr Mookerjee, echoing Sardar Patel's suggestions, bluntly called for Pakistan to cede territory if it could not protect its minorities. This was anathema to Nehru who would in the months to come go all out to try and gag Dr Mookerjee from reiterating this demand which had begun receiving huge public traction. Dr Mookerjee said,

> We should make a demand for one-third of the territory of Eastern Pakistan. In fact, I re-echo what Sardar Patel said in Nagpur about one and a half years ago. We must tell them: if you turn out one-third of the population from Eastern Bengal, pray give us one-third of your territory.... The reply to that is that is that supposing there are four crores of Muslims in India who wish to go away and Pakistan wants one-eighth of the territory of India, then what shall we do? I may say that that question does not arise. We are not asking Muslims to go. We are not. We shall make it possible for them to stay, if they wish to do so. If it is known that this problem is going to be settled honourably, favourably and justly, then the Hindus here, barring a few here and there, will stand by the Muslims—the mass population of Hindus will do that.

Besides undertaking extensive tours and interactions of the districts in West Bengal and Assam which had seen an influx of refugees, Dr Mookerjee mobilized efforts for their rehabilitation. Dr Mookerjee's efforts were not isolated nor were they undertaken only by his newly formed party Jana Sangh. His efforts at mobilizing public and political opinion in support of the minorities in East Bengal received wide support.

In November 1952, he convened an East Bengal Minorities Convention in the historic Calcutta University Institute

Hall. The Convention saw participation by parties such as Acharya Kripalani's Praja Socialist Party, the Hindu Mahasabha, the Revolutionary Socialist Party, Jana Sangh, Forward Bloc, RCPI, SRP [Socialist Republican Party], and the Bolshevik Party of West Bengal. Except for the Congress and communist party, all parties responded to Dr Mookerjee's call and came together 'on a common platform for a national cause'. It also showed the sweeping acceptance that Dr Mookerjee commanded even after his resignation from the Nehru cabinet. Sucheta Kripalani, a freedom fighter, Gandhian, and PSP leader and Member of Parliament, who was president of the Convention, minded new words when she said, 'Let there be no repetition of the old drama – exodus from Pakistan, agitation in India, tour by the Prime Minister in the affected area, a few lakh rupees granted for fresh relief work and quiet acceptance by the Government and the people of the squeezing out of minorities.' Dr Rammanohar Lohia also addressed the Convention. The All-Parties' Convention, among other things, 'unanimously demanded imposition of economic sanctions on Pakistan and stoppage of the supply of essential goods as a first step to put effective pressure on Pakistan to make her behave as a responsible Government'. It said,

> Addressing a huge public meeting at the conclusion of the Convention in Wellington Square, Kolkata, Dr Mookerjee argued that it was 'not physical suffering or deprivation of material wealth that aggravates the situation, it is a sense of helplessness, of daily fear of molestation and dishonour, of uprooting of all social and religious sentiments that corrodes the minds of the sufferers. This moral death is more piteous and tragic than the physical death'.

Meanwhile in New Delhi, addressing the press on the same day, Prime Minister Nehru casually asserted that 'apart from the minority community who were not happy, the situation in East Pakistan was more or less normal'. It was vintage Nehru—he had to obfuscate and minimize the reality so that his Pact with Pakistan could be salvaged at any cost. A few days after the All-Parties' Convention on the East Bengal Minorities, Dr Mookerjee addressed a large public meeting at the Park Circus Maidan in Kolkata, a central area in the city populated by minorities. 'A large number of Muslims attended it' and Dr Mookerjee frankly appealed to them to 'support the stand taken by the All-Parties' Convention'. The Pakistan government, he told the large gathering, 'had turned out to be an enemy of humanity and it was the duty of every man, a Hindu or Muslim, to raise his voice of protest wherever humanity was oppressed'.

An appeal was issued to the public to 'observe November 23, as the All-India East Bengal Minority Rights Day, all over the country under the combined auspices of all the parties'. Interestingly, 'leaders of all the non-Congress and non-Communist Parties of the country', including Dr S.P. Mookerjee, Acharya Kripalani and Sucheta Kripalani, Master Tara Singh, General Mohan Singh, R.S. Ruikar, leading lights of the All India Forward Bloc, S.S. More of the Peasants and Workers Party, and P.N. Rajbhoj of the All India Scheduled Castes Federation signed the appeal. This reveals the wide support the Hindus of East Bengal received from a wide cross-section of political opinion in India.

In another historic intervention in Lok Sabha on 15 November 1952, Dr Mookerjee appealed to Nehru not to underestimate the conditions of the Hindus by making such statements as:

everything is all right except some insecurity. For heaven's sake, do not say things which are not true. That will be like throwing salt into the gaping wound. You may not be able to protect them, you may not be able to help them, but do not minimize the gravity of the situation.... Find out an effective solution by which these people can be enabled to live exercising their elementary rights without being ruined as refugees or beggars or slaves.

The Nehru government, he said, was 'running away from the real problem'. On 23 November, the All-India East Bengal Minority Rights Day was observed throughout India. Jana Sangh had succeeded in bringing together a number of political parties to champion the issue. Dr Mookerjee addressed a mammoth public meeting at New Delhi's Ramlila Maidan along with leaders from the opposition and parties and groups in Parliament. Forward Bloc leader General Mohan Singh presided over the meeting. 'History,' Dr Mookerjee told the gathering, 'afforded no other example of recognising separate nationality based on the religion of a section of a country's population and sacrificing the cherished right of eight million people who passionately believed in United India.' What was needed was a 'full and frank re-survey of the situation and not the adoption of an ostrich-like attitude. Inaction or appeasement in such circumstances was neither dignified nor honourable but cowardly and hypocritical'.

Pandit Nehru's attitude and that of his communist comrades' were exactly this—cowardly and hypocritical. Dr Mookerjee exhorted Nehru:

Find a solution, a solution consistent with courage, with national prestige and with our national dignity. It is not a communal question. Why bring this Hindu-Muslim question into this? It is the Hindus who are suffering. Hindus as a race must live and it is not communal if you work for this end…. We claim to be a civilised democratic state, where people will have equal rights no matter what their religion is. But that does not mean we will allow Pakistan to play havoc with Hindu lives and honour and destroy the peace and stability of India.

But Nehru was obsessed only with his prestige and with his Pact with Pakistan which ultimately left the question, condition and future of minorities in Pakistan open-ended and unresolved.

The Bengali Hindu refugees were the worst sufferers of Nehru's false prestige and the communist's false politics. Blinded by the exigencies of vote-bank politics, the Congress, the communist parties and the later splinters like the TMC have ignored, opposed, or obfuscated the challenges and tribulations of the Bengali Hindu refugees. The communists have a record of massacring Bengali Hindu refugees, especially Dalit refugees who had come from East Bengal and wanted to settle down in West Bengal in the Sunderban estuary region of Marichjhapi.

These parties have always stood in the way of conferring dignity to the Bengali Hindus who have been compelled, forced, and terrorized to leave their homes and come away to India. Not to grant them citizenship today, to oppose their right to a life of dignity as citizens of India, will be to renege on a historic commitment. It will be ignoring their historic contribution to the making of a free India.

One cannot ignore the decades of suffering that these people underwent in their land of birth and also the miserable lives that they had been forced to lead as refugees in West Bengal and other parts of India. These people do not seek mercy, they do not seek favours—they aspire to a life of respect, of opportunities, and of a new horizon. India is their natural home, and they are entitled to seek a life of new hope here.

Syama Prasad's words in Parliament, describing the plight of the refugees and their will to survive, still rings:

> They are facing the spectre of death, not for any fault of their own. They cannot get shelter and they cannot get work. They do not want to live as idlers and it is amazing how even today, they raise their feeble voice and shout *Bande Mataram* which they have not forgotten yet and shed tears...

That justice and fair play came into being with the passage of the historic Citizenship Amendment Bill under the leadership of Prime Minister Narendra Modi and deftly argued for and piloted by Home Minister Amit Shah. A historic wrong was rectified; a historic commitment was fulfilled.

While placing the Bill in the Lok Sabha on 9 December 2019, Amit Shah articulated the essential points that defined the spirit in which the promise was finally being fulfilled. 'Afghanistan and Pakistan have clearly named Islam as their state religion,' he said and 'Bangladesh was formed as a secular country but was later designated an Islamic country. This closes the possibility of minority communities getting justice in these countries.' In the past, 'Pakistan had assured India that it would take care of its minorities, but it did not turn out that way,' Shah said while emphasizing that there will 'be no discrimination on the basis of religion'. However, India, he said, 'will not be quiet if such discrimination based on religion takes place in other neighbouring countries'. He also asked a fundamental question that most opinion-makers, leaders, and intellectuals have refused to ask: 'Minority populations reduced in neighbouring countries, where did they go?' This was a question that no one wanted to address; it made most uncomfortable. The truth was a gaping hole which most wanted to avoid looking into. 'The persecuted cannot be called infiltrators, they have come to us by fleeing,' he told the House.

For decades, the Congress and the communists opposed looking at the issue from this angle. They wanted to steam-roll the truth for the exigencies and pressures of the vote bank on which their politics propped itself and survived. The illegal infiltrator was more precious to them than the persecuted minority from India's neighbourhood. The former they patronized and the latter they silenced into submission. They repeatedly sacrificed the fate and the future of minorities in India's neighbourhood at the altar of false and self-serving politics. The passing of the CAA had not only overturned that but had also exposed their opportunism.

This reflection attempts to look at the historical context of the Citizenship Amendment Act and its various dimensions and debates against a wide political and historical backdrop. It relives the agonies and tribulations of a past that was sought to be blacked out or marginalized.

1

Pak Army Genocide and Exodus of Hindus in 1971

An Overlooked Chapter

Prime Minister (PM) Modi's address on 17 March 2020 on the occasion of the inauguration of Mujib Barsha (Mujib Year) to celebrate the centenary of Bangabandhu Sheikh Mujibur Rehman was an inspiring one. Recalling the struggle of the people of Bangladesh under the leadership of Bangabandhu, Modi observed 'how a repressive and cruel regime, disregarding all democratic values, unleashed a reign of injustice on "Bangla Bhumi" and devastated its people' and how Mujib 'had devoted every moment of his life towards bringing Bangladesh out of the phase of devastation and genocide and making it a positive and progressive society'.

Referring to Bangladesh's trajectory of becoming a confident and progressive nation today, making steady progress on all development indexes, PM Modi drew attention to the stark contrast between two nations—Pakistan and Bangladesh. 'We are all witnessing,' he observed, 'that how, making terror and violence weapons of politics and diplomacy destroys a society and a nation. The world is also watching where the supporters of terror and violence are currently placed and in what state they are, while Bangladesh is scaling new heights.' Modi pointed out the stark reality, which is that of Pakistan—a half-nation subsisting on terror and violence and Bangladesh—a nation which is steadily and maturely moving towards stability, development, and economic growth. Modi himself has done much in bringing about greater stability in the area, and has, over the last few years, steered the focus towards the vision of shared development and collective well-being in the region.

At a time when the debate on citizenship and the granting of citizenship to minorities who have faced persecution in India's neighbourhood raged and a number of myopic half-truths were being dished out on why citizenship must be denied to this section, it is relevant to look at this phase of 1971, which saw one of the largest tranches of refugees come into India of which the majority were Bengali Hindus, and as many as 90 per cent were Hindus. The minority population of East Pakistan in 1971 was around 16–17 per cent and the bulk of those driven out by the Pak army composed of them. In his deeply disturbing masterpiece, *Blood Telegram: India's Secret War in East Pakistan* (2013), American journalist Gary Bass notes how India had 'secretly recorded that by the middle of June, there were some 5,330,000 Hindus, as against 443,000 Muslims and 150,000 from other groups'. A number of Indian diplomats, notes Bass, 'believed that the Hindus would be too afraid ever to go back' to East Pakistan. Bass also records in some detail the role that Senator Edward Kennedy played in exposing the Pakistan army's genocide in East Pakistan during those crucial months. Kennedy played a crucial role in highlighting the Pak army's perfidy to the world. He undertook tours to refugee camps in West Bengal and Tripura. Bass narrates Kennedy's heart-rending tours and his interactions with these hapless refugees. Touring the northern fringes of Kolkata during those fateful days, Kennedy met dozens of Bengali peasants who narrated their harrowing tales; they were a few samples of the actual exodus, and Kennedy saw 'children dying along the road as their parents pleaded for help. Many were obviously in shock, sitting in despair by the side of the road wandering blindly. Most of them, he realised, were Hindus'.

In a statement he issued on 1 November 1971, Edward Kennedy wrote:

Field reports to the US Government, countless eye-witnesses, journalistic accounts, reports of International agencies such as the World Bank and additional information available to the subcommittee document the reign of terror which grips East Bengal (East Pakistan). Hardest hit have been members of the Hindu community who have been robbed of their lands and shops, systematically slaughtered, and in some cases, painted with yellow patches marked 'H'. All of this has been officially sanctioned, ordered and implemented under martial law from Islamabad. The mandate of the Pakistani Army was to 'kill Hindus'. The collaborators within East Pakistan, such as the razakars and al-badars, helped to locate Hindu homes and businesses, marking them with a yellow H.

The passing of the CAA, thus, was an attempt to bring to closure this devastating episode; it was meant to give permanency of existence as citizens of India to these persecuted people. The Pakistan army and establishment, ever since its formation in 1947, had been systematically carrying out pogroms against its Hindu minorities, especially in its eastern wing. These gradual, systematic, and periodic pogroms and Pakistan's driving out minorities have been documented over the years. It is this that kept the citizenship debate alive in India. Should not the beleaguered minorities of Pakistan be protected and given shelter, space, and scope in India as promised in the past, or should they be left at the mercy of the Islamic state of Pakistan, which does not believe in providing equity to its minorities?

Many of those in the West who have been persisting with their fallacious hectoring of India on the citizenship issue and have continued to do so over the years, soon after the CAA was passed as law by the Indian Parliament, are supporters and patrons of Pakistan and its diabolically destabilizing policies. They stood by it or silently looked the other way when Pakistan was indulging in planned pogroms against its minorities and when the Pakistan army was perpetrating one of the worst genocides against its own citizens in the eastern wing, butchering intellectuals and mowing down the Hindu minorities. Veteran journalist D.R. Mankekar notes in *Colonialism in East Bengal* (1971):

> Senior military and civil officers in Dacca and Comilla repeatedly told Mascarenhas [Anthony Mascarenhas, journalist, who fled Pakistan, and filed his stories from London on the Pak army's genocide]: 'We are determined to cleanse East Pakistan once and for all of the threat of secession, even if it means killing off two million people and ruling the province as a colony for 30 years'.

In his now famous and historic article, written in the *Sunday Times* from London, Mascarenhas has noted how Pakistanis elaborated their policy towards its eastern wing thus:

> 1) Bengalis have proved themselves 'unreliable' and must be ruled by West Pakistanis, 2) The Bengalis will have to be re-educated along proper Islamic lines. The 'Islamisation of the masses' is intended to eliminate secessionist tendencies and provide a strong religious bond with West Pakistan, 3) When the Hindus have been eliminated by death and flight, their property will be bait to win over the Muslim middle class. This will provide the base for erecting administrative and political structures in the future.

This was the blood-thirsty, false ideology-driven agenda of the theocratic state of Pakistan.

One of those who witnessed the era first-hand and played a crucial role in the historic events of that period was P.N. Dhar, a diplomat administrator and the advisor to Indira Gandhi. In his memoirs, Dhar, a Kashmiri pandit, notes how, when the Pakistan army genocide began, the 'first to arrive were the Awami League cadres and remnants of the police and the military personnel who managed to escape. They were followed by Hindus who had escaped a merciless hunt'. It was only in the middle of April 1971 that Indian authorities understood the design of Pakistan in unleashing the genocide, writes Dhar:

> By driving out the Hindus in their millions, they hoped to substantially reduce the political support that the Awami League enjoyed as it was the 'wily Hindu' who was supposed to have misled simple Bengali Muslims into demanding

autonomy. Additionally with the Hindus gone, Bengal would lose its majority status *vis-a-vis* West Pakistan and not be in a position to challenge its dominance. (2000)

This indoctrination against Hindus in East Pakistan had started in the early days of Partition and percolated all layers of society. The Pakistani regime's perpetual anti-India stance was placed before the people as a perpetual struggle against a 'Hindu' India, as a 'broad struggle against Hindus, the adherents of a religion', writes Pakistani politician-academic Farahanaz Ispahani. The acerbic Dawn, for instance, after India's liberation of the Portuguese-occupied enclave of Goa, wrote in its editorial that as soon as India is confident enough, 'she will try to wipe out Pakistan because Indians in their heart still regard the areas now forming Pakistan as basically parts of *Akhand Bharat* over which some day Hindu rule must extend'. This mindset and approach were also the driving idea of Pakistan since its demand and formation.

In the early days after its formation, the Islamist lobby—driven and dominated by the Mullahs—made it clear that Pakistan had to become a completely Islamic state. The Munir Commission, set up by the Pakistan government in 1953, to examine the state of religious intolerance in Pakistan, extensively interviewed these Islamist leaders and ulemas and noted that they were determined that the position of non-Muslims in Pakistan 'will be that of *dhimmis* and they will not be full citizens of Pakistan because they will not have the same rights as Muslims'. It was this fundamentalist orthodox mindset which persecuted and drove out the minorities from East Pakistan in waves after 1947. A voluminous report by a group of eminent Indian jurists in 1965 on the recurring exodus of minorities from East Pakistan pointing at this trend mentioned how 'right from the beginning discrimination against the non-Muslims became the rule' in East Pakistan and how 'the Muslim League government in East Pakistan let loose a reign of terror on Hindus' utilizing 'police and goondas'.

Ayub Khan's rule (1958–69), for instance, saw 'Islamic Studies' in Pakistan made compulsory for grades six to eight. The syllabus, writes Ispahani, 'emphasised Islam's martial traditions', harped on a 'long-standing conflict between Hindus and Muslims in the subcontinent (2015)' and hammered into the students that Pakistan 'was created to be an Islamic state'. This repeated emphasis and reiteration of Pakistan's 'Islamic ideology', argues Ispahani, 'contributed substantially to the periodic emigration of Bengali Hindus to India' (ibid.).

A study of Pakistani textbooks reveals the creative levels of this indoctrination, for example, 'the nation is identified with the Muslim community. The basis of the nation is the profession of faith itself (*kalima*). To be a good Moslem means to be a patriot. Islam and nation are synonymous'. In a history textbook describing the formation of Pakistan, the narrator is dramatically the Minar-e-Pakistan itself, standing at the spot in Lahore from where the Muslim League had passed the Pakistan resolution in 1940, and speaking of how in an independent India, Muslims would have been subjugated and treated as untouchables by Hindus: 'They would have set up a government where the laws of the Hindus would have been in force rather than the laws of God, by which the Muslims would have been untouchables.' The textbooks falsely spoke of Muslims being the victims of Partition and being killed by Hindus.

It was this sort of continuous indoctrination right from the primary level that led to further consolidation of an anti-Hindu mindset against the Hindus of East Pakistan and led to their constant branding as 'agents of India'. The Hindu population in East Pakistan, which constituted an 'influential 20 per cent of the province's population in the 1951 census had fallen to just 12 per cent by the time of the 1961 census'. It is the depletion of Hindus from East Pakistan which saw the ranks of refugees in India, especially in bordering states, mostly West Bengal, swell.

Bass, for instance, records how the then Indian Foreign Minister Swaran Singh, in a briefing for Indian diplomats, agitatedly divulged how the Pakistan army was mowing down its own civilians:

> Artillery, tanks, automatic weapons, mortars, aeroplanes, everything which is normally used against invading armed forces, were utilised and very large-scale killings took place; selective killings of individuals, acts of molestation and rape against the university students, girls, picking out the Awami League leaders, their supporters and later on especially concentrating on the localities in which Hindus predominated. (2013)

The New York Times, strangely in reports then, unlike now when it is at the forefront of opposing the granting of Indian citizenship to Hindu refugees, would relate the truth. This was mainly because of the Pulitzer Prize-winning journalist Sydney Schanberg who immortalized the descriptions of this phase through his reports filed against great odds. Schanberg's report 'West Pakistan Pursues Subjugation of Bengalis' filed on 13 July, noted,

Although the targets were Bengali Moslems and the 10 million Hindus at first, the army, is now concentrating on Hindus in what foreign observers characterize as a holy war. The West Pakistani leaders have long, considered the Hindus as subverters of Islam they now view them as agents of India, which, has been accused of engineering the autonomy movement to force Pakistan's disintegration. Of the more than six million Bengalis who are believed to have fled to India to escape the army's terror, at least four million are Hindus. The troops are still killing Hindus and burning and looting their villages. (1971)

Earlier, on 29 June 1971, writing from Faridpur, Schanberg recorded how the Pakistani Army 'has painted big yellow "H's" on the Hindu shops still standing in this town to identify the property of the minority eighth of the population that it has made its special targets' (ibid.). This particular and oft-cited report describes the situation that the Bengali Hindus faced at the hands of the Pakistan Army—how they faced persecution, extermination, and an uncertain existence.

Schanberg noted how 'an undetermined number of Faridpur's 10,000 Hindus have been killed and others have fled across the border to predominantly Hindu India'. Some of them were also seen returning from India. This was not, as Schanberg argued, 'out of faith in a change of heart by the army but rather out of despair. They do not want to live as displaced persons in India and they feel that nowhere in East Pakistan is really safe for them, so they would rather be unsafe in their own town'. His story of an old woman and her 84-year-old husband who wanted to stay in 'golden Bengal' remains especially unnerving:

A 70-year-old Hindu woman who was shot through the neck said that as bad as conditions were and as frightened as she was, 'this is our home—we want to stay in golden Bengal.' On April 21, when the army rolled into Faridpur, the old woman and her 84-year-old husband ran to seek refuge in a Hindu village, Bodidangi, about three miles away. The next day the army hit Bodidangi and, reliable local reports say, as many as 300 Hindus were massacred. The old woman stumbled and fell as she tried to flee Bodidangi, she related, and two soldiers caught her. She said they beat her, ripped off her jewellery, fired a shot at point blank range into her neck and left her for dead. She and her husband had owned a small piece of property on which they rented out a few flimsy huts. Only the dirt floors are left, she said.

The Pakistan Army's campaign against the Hindu minorities was a systematic one. As Schanberg recorded, 'Soldiers fanned through virtually every village asking where the Hindus lived.' Hindu properties were confiscated, sold, or 'given' to 'loyal' citizens; many of the beneficiaries of this largesse were 'Biharis, non-Bengali Muslim migrants from India', most of whom worked with the army. The army, wrote Schanberg, 'has given weapons to a large number of the Biharis, and it is they who have often continued the killing of Hindus in areas where the army has eased off'. The Hindus were financially victimized as well. Schanberg noted that 'Hindu bank accounts are frozen. Almost no Hindu students or teachers have returned to the schools.'

In a report, published on 21 September titled 'Bengali Refugees Say Soldiers Continue to Kill, Loot and Burn', from a border village in West Bengal, which saw a huge influx of refugees from East Pakistan, Schanberg wrote,

The refugees said that although general living conditions were very difficult in East Pakistan, they would have stayed had it not been for the killings. Nearly all the latest arrivals are Hindus, who said that the military regime was still making the Hindu minority its particular target. They said the guerrillas were active in their areas and that the army carried out massive reprisals against civilians after every guerrilla raid. Nira Pada Saha, a jute trader in Faridpur District, told of reprisal against a village near his that had sheltered and fed the guerrillas. Just before he fled five days ago, he related, the army struck the village, first shelling it and then burning the huts. 'Some of the villagers didn't run away fast enough,' he said. 'The soldiers caught them, tied their hands and feet and threw them into the flames.' There were about 5,000 people in the village, most of them Hindus, Mr. Saha said, and not [a person] is left. (1971)

In another report filed on 10 October, 'East Pakistani Town in Guerrilla Enclave Is Coming Back to Life', from an enclave in East Pakistan that had been liberated from the Pak army's grip by the guerrillas of the Mukti Bahini, Schanberg observed how most of the villagers of Putkhali came back except the Hindus:

The villagers began to come back, slowly at first and then in larger numbers, so that the population has grown to 1,400—almost normal, except for the absent Hindus, who have been special targets of the Moslem troops. Not one of the several Hindu families from the village has returned from India, and people do not think they ever will.

An American who was in Dhaka from March to April 1971, in a twenty-four-page report that he sent back

to America, noted that what was happening in Dhaka
under the Pak army was perhaps 'one of history's most
massive examples of genocide'. Moving around Dhaka on
27 March after the curfew had been lifted, he described the
scene: 'The whole area (in Old Dacca), largely inhabited by
the Hindu community was cordoned off and burned and its
inhabitants machine-gunned in the streets.' Describing the
visits by the American, Mankekar writes,

> The American visited the ruins of two Hindu temples in the
> centre of the Ramna racetrack near the Intercontinental
> Hotel. The Pakistani army has sacked the two places of
> worship. 'The old walls of the temple had been breached,
> apparently the work of a tank,' he wrote down. 'I saw what
> was described to me as being a pit filled with bodies.'

Hendrik Vander Heidjen, economist and member of
the World Bank Mission, who was on a tour in some
parts of East Bengal, spoke of 'an awesome panorama of
destruction and damage – with people looking terrified,
shocked and dazed … was like the morning after a nuclear
attack….' Heidjen wrote of how during his visit to Phultala
in Khulna, 'fifty percent of the population' of the thana—
police station—had fled; 'Some 20,000 of 42,000 mostly
Hindus, leaving behind unattended plots of lands, houses,
etc., everything had been disrupted there: the livestock
officer had been killed, the whole administration was in
chaos, the people bewildered…'

The genocidal tentacles of the Pak army were especially
aimed at 'liquidating Hindus'. Mankekar wrote,

> Kill as many Hindus as possible, and drive the rest to India,
> that seems to be their mandate. That way the Pakistani

rulers would simultaneously be solving East Bengal's political and demographic problems ... Islamabad is now planning to transplant the immigrant Muslim population from West Pakistan to fill the vacuum in East Wing. (1971)

This cleansing of Hindus in erstwhile East Bengal and East Pakistan had begun the day Pakistan was formed. The persecution, genocide, and fight continued over the decades till it reached a bloody crescendo in 1971. Pravash Chandra Lahiry, a freedom fighter, member of the East Pakistan Assembly, and once minister of finance in East Pakistan, gives an insight into the plight of the Hindus during the 1950s and 1960s, and how in the 'administrative sphere also, the Government of Pakistan' followed a 'consistent and persistent' policy of 'invidious distinction between the Hindus and Muslims'. Representation of the minority community in the Civil Service of Pakistan and the Junior Civil Service and Police Service was almost nil. 'Employment in other grades of services is most unsatisfactory. The ratio of minority representation in service is observed more in breaches than in observances. The doors of non-government and semi-government offices are practically closed to the minorities (1964).' Lahiry rued:

[In every sphere of life] the minorities are hounded out to take the penalty of following a 'Faith' other than 'Islam.' The Muslim League leaders have been seeing everything through their coloured glasses of communalism and enacting laws even, either to reduce them to the status of second-class citizenship or to squeeze them out to India, only to make Pakistan a homogenous state of the Muslims alone.... The Government of Pakistan have left no stone unturned to avail of the opportunities of

squeezing out the Hindus by contriving all possible
devices of their own.... Pakistan has been consistently
and persistently following a policy of hatred and
discrimination among its own people.... The State of
Pakistan was brought into being on hatred of India and
the Hindus and it is, therefore, the sheet-anchor of its
policy of administration to continue the same policy for
its preservation. (ibid.)

These events and policies led to the showdown of 1971.
While Bangladesh was created as a separate country with
Bengali language and culture as its sustaining layer, the
Hindus of Bangladesh, especially after the assassination of
Sheikh Mujib and the rise of parties controlled by Pakistan
and owing allegiance to it, continued to face persecution at
the hands of the Bangladesh Nationalist Party, the Jamaat,
and other fundamentalist and radical groups.

It is interesting to recall, in this context, how the
Bharatiya Jana Sangh (BJS), the progenitor of the Bharatiya
Janata Party and founded by the Bengali educationist-
statesman Dr Syama Prasad Mookerjee, was at the forefront
of demanding a free Bangladesh. Led by Atal Bihari
Vajpayee in Parliament, the BJS also launched a countrywide movement in support of the demand.

Atal Bihari Vajpayee, in a passionate intervention,
speaking in the Lok Sabha on 18 June 1971 in support of a
resolution moved by Samar Guha, Netaji's political disciple,
freedom fighter and Forward Bloc leader, who had himself
left East Bengal as a refugee, described the situation in East
Pakistan, 'The political solutions about which we are talking
means that the Government of elected representatives of
Bangladesh should be established there, Bangladesh should

cease to be a colony, the refugees who have fled could return and their life, property and honour may remain secure.'

In an impassioned plea, Vajpayee called for the Government of India to raise the issue of genocide in East Pakistan in the UN; there can be only one policy for India, Vajpayee argued, that was to make a firm resolve 'not to compromise with the present position and to create conditions in Bangladesh whereby displaced persons could return to their homes and democracy could be established there (Ghatate 1996)'. For that to happen, Vajpayee told the House, 'If there is no alternative except war India should get ready for war.'

Ten days later, speaking on the 'holocaust in Bangladesh' and 'liberation as the only solution', Vajpayee movingly spoke of the need for India to go for it alone, if need be, and not dither:

> If we have to go it alone, we will go ahead. Bangladesh is a country of Rabindra Nath Tagore and Kazi Nazrul Islam. Poet Rabindra had told us: *'Ekla chalo re, Yadi tor dak sune keu na ashe, Tabe ekla chalo re.'* So let us walk alone on the path of duty, go alone for the defence of democracy in Bangladesh. We are not bound to preserve the unity of Pakistan. (ibid.)

In June 1971, Vajpayee was already referring to East Pakistan as 'Bangladesh'. In July 1971, in its all-India session held in Udaipur, the Jana Sangh, speaking of rendering 'immediate help to Bangladesh', called on the Indira government to accord immediate recognition to the 'democratically elected Government of Swadhin Bangladesh' and to provide it with 'effective moral and material help' and to make efforts for the 'early release of Sheikh Mujibur Rehman and others under arrest'. Referring to Pakistan as a 'monstrous absurdity', the Jana Sangh also demanded that 'effective curbs be put on Sheikh Abdullah, Majlis-e-Mushawrat, Tamir-e-Millat and Jamait-e-Islam, Muslim League and other elements that have consistently refused to condemn the [Pakistan] military junta for its genocide in Bangladesh'.

In subsequent weeks and months, Jana Sangh launched countrywide political programmes in order to educate public opinion and garner public support for the recognition of Bangladesh. A look at the resolutions, debates and descriptions of these programmes indicates the massive drive the Jana Sangh undertook in support of the formation of Bangladesh. In August 1971, it launched the Bangladesh Satyagraha month for the recognition of Bangladesh. Twenty-eight thousand 'satyagrahis' courted arrest; among them was a young twenty-year-old *satyagrahi*, Narendra Modi, who would eventually rise to lead India as Prime Minister. BJS stalwarts such as Vajpayee, Bhai Mahavir, P. Parameswaran, Sunder Singh Bhandari, Nana Deshmukh, Pitamber Das, Balraj Madhok, Bacchraj Vyas, among others, led the *satyagrahi*s at various places. Delhi, Uttar Pradesh, Madhya Pradesh, Maharashtra, Rajasthan, Bihar, Haryana, West Bengal, Mysore, Jammu & Kashmir, Kerala, and Andhra Pradesh, among other states, saw a large participation in the satyagraha for recognising 'Swadhin Bangladesh'.

The Jana Sangh was unrelenting in pressuring India to recognize Bangladesh. This episode of the history of Bangladesh's liberation has not been adequately highlighted. While the BJS consistently demanded the rehabilitation of and citizenship for Bengali Hindu refugees who were driven out of East Pakistan and called out Pak genocide against Hindus, it was also active in supporting the demand for Bangladesh. Despite being in opposition, it supported Indira Gandhi's government in its action to liberate Bangladesh and mobilized countrywide opinion in support of the creation of Bangladesh.

The majority of Hindu refugees who had been evicted from East Pakistan in 1971 never went back. They never could as their homes and hearth were destroyed and their faith forever crushed. To make things worse, they had to eke out an existence in India. The CAA is also meant for them. Those who oppose it have conveniently forgotten or have deliberately ignored that aspect. One hardly ever hears a discussion on these historic dimensions and the need to address and settle these issues.

P.N. Luthra, of the Indian Civil Service, who worked throughout his life on refugee rehabilitation and possessed a vast knowledge of India's northeast, described this massive influx of 1971, generated because of the Pakistan army's genocidal policies, as follows:

> However poignant the record of refugee tragedies has been, none of them come to the level of what the world has witnessed in the way of the refugee influx which started on the fatal day of March 26, 1971 [a day after the Pak army's crackdown on students and intellectuals at Dhaka University] from East Bengal. Its number has surpassed any other displacement from a single country. The nature and magnitude of this influx is unique in history. (1971)

Having closely worked on refugee rehabilitation for most of his life and possessing a knack for documenting his experiences, Luthra's description of the refugee movement is perhaps among the most authentic. Of the manner in which the refugees were pouring into India, Luthra wrote about how they were entering India from 'numerous points' along thousands of miles of the border: 'They are utilising all modes of transport such as bullock carts, motor cars, country boats, rickshaws and the like.' But the majority trod 'long distances on foot in grim agony and in a desperate effort to escape from the ruthless atrocities of the Pakistan Army' (ibid.). Even seven months after the Pak army's crackdown, observed Luthra, 'the influx continues at an enormous rate' (ibid.). Bengali Hindus were special targets of the Pak army.

While Sheikh Hasina's government has held a bold and exemplary War Crimes trial against Razakar collaborators of the Pakistan army's genocide in Bangladesh, *Mujib Barsha* (2020–2021), the 50th anniversary of the Bangladesh Liberation War, was the right time to call for an international trial of the Pakistani army itself for its role in war crimes and genocide in 1971.

The self-styled international 'conscience keepers' of the world must respond. The saga of the entire citizenship narrative in India, the Bangladesh Liberation War, and the genocidal atrocities of the Pakistan Army fifty years ago are intertwined. In India, some continue to maintain a silence on this gruesome and disturbing episode of contemporary history, while in Bangladesh some continue to lament the defeat of Pakistan in 1971.

2

'We Will All Sink'

How Nehru Dumped Bengali Hindu Refugees

Nehru's attitude towards the Bengali Hindu refugees and the Hindus of East Bengal is best illustrated by Dr Rammanohar Lohia. Lohia referred to a conversation he had with Nehru sometime towards the end of 1946 in Noakhali. 'Mr Nehru spoke of the water, slime, bush and tree that he found everywhere in East Bengal,' Lohia recalled, 'He said that was not the India he or I knew and wanted with some vehemence to cut East Bengal away from the main land of India. That was an extraordinary observation' (2000). Speaking of himself, Lohia averred, 'I have found the gay laughter of East Bengal women unparalleled in all the world.'

This inability to understand East Bengal contributed to Nehru's aversion to standing by the Hindus of East Bengal. Of Nehru's capacities and his leadership, historian Prafulla Chakrabarti caustically argued,

Nehru had the limited vision of a nineteenth-century liberal and he was out of his depth in the storm-tossed sea which was India after partition. The abdication of

Gandhi had set the Indian political stage for a starry-eyed Cambridge don to experiment with his mental constructs with the wilfulness of a spoilt child.... Nehru was too finicky, too conscious of his image as a democratic man of peace projected before the world. He had the degenerate orthodoxy of the self-sufficient English liberal. Socialism was a fashion of his early youth like the familiar rose in his buttonhole. (1999)

Nehru's attitude to Bengali Hindu refugees remained confused throughout his years in office. For instance, he tried to explain their persecution and displacement in such words: 'Entirely voluntary, of course voluntary in the sense that there is a process of circumstance; people are not pushed out except by circumstances' (March 1950). Only Nehru could interpret or explain what he meant by these words which were the product of a convoluted logic.

Pandit Lakshmi Kanta Maitra, legendary leader of the Congress from Bengal, member of the Constituent Assembly, later member of parliament from Nabadvip in the first Lok Sabha, and more importantly for us, a close elder friend of Dr Syama Prasad Mookerjee, who stood by him in his herculean efforts to provide succour and stand by the beleaguered minorities of East Bengal, forcefully spoke in Parliament during a discussion on 17 March 1950.

In January that year, Pakistan launched a premeditated pogrom against its minorities. A continuous stream and, at times, a flood of Bengali Hindus, who had been uprooted in Pakistan, began moving towards West Bengal and Assam. The discussion centred on that deeply unsettling issue. One needs to specially look at this phase, primarily because this was the second starting point of the exodus that brought about the enactment of the Citizenship Amendment Act.

Nehru, speaking on those left behind in East Bengal, told the House that 'first of all the minorities in East Bengal [later East Pakistan] are certainly our concern to the extent that they have security, and if they do not have security, measures will have to be devised to give them security' (ibid.). Panditji was also emphatic:

> [That] those who have suffered be helped in every way, rehabilitated and compensated, that an intensified search should be made for looted property and that those persons found in possession of it and who have not voluntarily returned it would be considered guilty of having looted it and punished accordingly. (ibid.)

Nehru also spoke of the 'abduction of women and to forced conversions' and 'that forced conversions will not be recognised and that every attempt will be made to recover women who might have been abducted.' As he had always done, especially when it came to addressing the effects of the partition on the eastern front, Nehru soon forgot this promise.

Nehru's sense and feeling of the excruciating trials and tribulations of the refugees, especially of those who were pouring in from East Bengal, was stunted and halting. He could not offer any concrete steps to be taken and had no immediate or long-term plan to mitigate their sufferings. He saw their suffering and narrated them in a cavalier manner but rarely could get into the thick of things and be their lead or provide a way out. As Chakrabarti noted, 'He did not breathe in deeply the particular aroma of the

Indian soil; did not share in the joys and sorrows, the superstitions and angularities, the loves and hates of the Indian people' and he had no 'sense of participation in their lives' (1999).

His description of the refugee influx after a visit to Ranaghat in Nadia is a case in point; it reveals his capacity to witness and not be involved, to see but not to lead:

> Some certificates were required of domicile or income tax; they are not necessary now. Some other difficulties arose at the Customs at one time and to some extent even now, the difficulties may be there. They had to pass through four barriers. The Customs barrier was legitimate; again, a police barrier; then the Ansar barrier and then a barrier of common folk who called themselves 'Janagana' that is people who gathered together. To some extent the people passed through these four barriers and lost some of their belongings at each barrier. However, I think this is lessening greatly now. I visited the day before yesterday a big camp at Ranaghat where these people are arriving daily—some arrived the day before yesterday and some earlier and they all arrived roughly about 10 or 12 days ago—and I had found that many of them have been able to bring a fair quantity of luggage with them, pots, pans, utensils, beddings and in some cases trunks. Obviously there had been a relaxation in people bringing goods, because I saw this luggage with them. What they were deprived of was mostly, I think, hard cash, which was taken away or which went in the shape of some kind of bribe given to the various people who stopped them, so that they might bring other goods with them.

There was no categorial assurance or answer—all these were taken care of and removed. To a question by Pandit

Maitra, regarding the jewellery that the refugees could or managed to bring with them, Nehru replied that he

> did see some women wearing gold bangles in the camps. Of course, I cannot say whether others, probably, were taken away; they may have been, but, at any rate, some wore gold bangles; I saw one or two with necklaces in their necks in the last few days because the people were coming home in the last ten days or so.

Maitra, in his intervention, exposed Pakistan's ruse, which anyone else would have seen through, except Jawaharlal Nehru. Maitra's was a heart-rending description and it also exposed how superficial Nehru's understanding was of the situation. We quote Maitra at some length:

> It is one thing to show or evince intellectual sympathy but it is another thing to heal the wounds of those who have suffered so grievously. The hon. Prime Minister said that while visiting Ranaghat, he found refugees able to carry luggage, bedding, etc. I do not challenge that. During the last few days when Pandit Jawaharlal Nehru visited Bengal, Pakistan became cautious. They knew quite well that the Prime Minister of India was sitting in Calcutta—was coming from Delhi to Calcutta off and on during the last eleven days and they took jolly good care to see that some people at least from some points were allowed to come over to India with some of their belongings. But there are numerous other points from which the people are simply trekking into the Indian territory from Pakistan and the versions that those people are giving us are that not only they are deprived of everything at every stage but their women-folk are taken away or dishonoured. Today I saw in the papers that women folk were subjected to such

atrocities; they were taken to secluded places where their relations were not allowed to go and they were subjected to all manner of indignities on the pretext of searching their persons. Letters are pouring in which describe these tales, which I have never known happening in the history of any country in the world; nowhere has there been such a large-scale dis-honour of women, large-scale abduction of women, mass rape and other indignities on womanhood. I do not know if the hon. Prime Minister enquired about that.

On Nehru's observations that women were coming in with their jewellery, Maitra bluntly told the prime minister that the country was so 'much perturbed over the happenings in Eastern Pakistan that kind of statement which the hon. Prime Minister has made will not remove the great uneasiness or assuage the feelings'. Maitra also assailed Nehru's attack on the Indian press and his dictate that the Indian press must observe restraint. On the contrary, Pandit Maitra pointed out that the Indian press was behaving most responsibly and acting with utmost restraint, restricting itself to the doles of information from the government's Press Information Bureau. But was it the Prime Minister's case, he wondered, 'that nothing should be published in this country, no news of what is happening in East Bengal—, nothing of the terrible happenings there should be allowed to see the light of day? Is that his contention?'

This was a few weeks before the Nehru–Liaquat Pact was inked. Nehru was convinced that he was about to come up with an ingenious framework of peace and told the House with a flourish that he intended to issue a joint statement with the Pakistan prime minister 'guaranteeing protection to minorities'. Leaders from West Bengal, with

Dr Syama Prasad Mookerjee in the lead, had already expressed their deep misgivings about the move. Dr Mookerjee, then a minister in the union cabinet, had expressed grave apprehensions that the pact or joint statement would be a non-starter. He would eventually resign over it.

But the world-statesman in Nehru refused to consider these arguments. In fact, Nehru possessed little understanding of or interest in the fate of the beleaguered Hindus coming in from East Bengal. Pandit Maitra spoke with great emotion and, among other things, asked a very pertinent question. He had, like Dr Mookerjee, anticipated the failure of this proposed joint statement and was among those leaders who were rooted to the soil and had not forsaken their sense of the grassroots for vague postures of internationalism. It is therefore important to know the positions of these great minds and public personalities from Bengal since the anti-CAA chorus was most shrill in that state and certain political parties were at the forefront of trying to deceive people and sidetrack them from the real issue. One also needs to recall Maitra's words, primarily because he was a pragmatic, rooted, and farsighted Congressman—a breed which is completely absent in the current Congress dispensation. Both Pandit Maitra and Dr Mookerjee could foresee what Nehru could not or refused to see.

On Nehru's proposed joint statement with Liaquat Ali Khan, Maitra retorted,

> I do not know what he really means. Does he really believe that any agreement, any undertaking or any covenant with India, that may be entered into with Pakistan, would be respected by it? Day after day questions have been raised on the floor of the House about the violation by Pakistan of

this or that agreement with India. It is absolutely clear that every single pact that Pakistan makes with India will be more honoured by it in the breach than in the observance.... Does he really believe that when all the offers that he made recently to Pakistan with a view to fact-finding with regard to disturbances in East Bengal were turned down, that any agreement if entered into now, would be respected by Pakistan? He suggested that the Prime Ministers of both the countries should jointly tour over the affected areas in both but Pakistan said 'No'. Two commissions from the two sides should visit the respective areas—'No'. The Red Cross Society people would tour over the affected areas— 'No'. Whatever the Prime Minister of India proposed to Pakistan has been turned down by it. I ask how does he honestly feel that if this joint declaration or statement that is contemplated by him is made, it will be implemented by Pakistan. This will only give it an opportunity to wriggle out of the present difficult position. I have not the least doubt that by doing this the Prime Minister instead of doing service to my province, service to the afflicted people, would be doing positive disservice.

Instead of applying a healing balm to the refugees who were anxiously waiting for the Prime Minister to alleviate their suffering, by declaring that he would firm up a pact with Pakistan, Jawaharlal Nehru had sprayed those 'lacerated hearts' with a 'saline water douche', Pandit Maitra lamented.

Maitra reminded the House how he had repeatedly warned it over the last two years that 'Pakistan is a professedly theocratic Islamic State' and, therefore, 'how on earth' could one 'rely on their sense of justice to protect the non-Muslim minorities?' If such an undertaking for protection of minorities was given by either side, Maitra argued, 'we will carry it out alright and we will do it with a vengeance. But I know very well – and any honest man in this House in his heart of hearts knows that whatever undertaking is given by the Pakistan Government will not be implemented by it.' An agreement at this stage, Maitra observed, will be a kind of step back and, in fact, further debilitate the sentiments and state of mind of the afflicted minorities; it will be akin to a 'saline water douche' on the 'lacerated hearts' of the beleaguered minorities who are being compelled to come away. Maitra pleaded that instead of generating false hopes, it would be infinitely more honest to say what Pakistan had said: '[That] Pakistan is a foreign territory and if its nationals are molested, it is no concern of ours in India. This would be infinitely more honest. Let us for God's sake not raise high hopes any longer. That is a danger and this will have very disastrous repercussions on the whole country.'

Maitra concluded by arguing that Muslims were not in danger in West Bengal, unlike the minorities in Pakistan, and therefore, the pact would be futile and only serve to raise false hopes in the minds of the Hindus in East Bengal. 'It is not the case that there has been any large-scale disturbance in West Bengal,' he told the House adding:

There is no doubt about the security which the Muslims enjoy in West Bengal. If it is said there is no security for Muslims in West Bengal, it is entirely wrong. I therefore feel that this Joint statement, which he [Nehru] proposes to make will, instead of helping the situation, create exasperation in the country, and it will make the task of those who are maintaining peace and order in the country extremely difficult. I again repeat that instead of raising any false hope, let him frankly say that the Government of India cannot do anything in the matter. That would be infinitely better than this kind of vague and indefinite thing.

Most, except Nehru, saw the futility of such a pact.

Nehru answered Maitra in a typical way by dismissing his apprehensions. It is interesting to sample the reply. Nehru said,

> I pointed out that in recent months there has been a certain flow of refugees. I referred to a certain declaration, whether it will be made or not, I do not know, it depends upon other factors. The other party has been repeating what we have been saying – whether they put it into practice or not is another matter.... That is my point, what Mr Lakshmi Kanta Maitra said was perfectly true and yet what I said was perfectly true. That is to say all those things have happened, but for the present things are not happening. Whether they will happen tomorrow or not is another matter.

This was Nehru's convoluted answer to Maitra's pointed question on whether he actually believed that Pakistan could be relied upon to look after the minorities who stayed back there.

Nehru's answer to K. Hanumanthaiya, one of the tallest leaders of Karnataka, was utterly crass and dismissive. Hanumanthaiya had argued in a strong and forceful intervention during the discussion that there ought to be a complete exchange of population on the eastern front, much in the line that Dr Mookerjee had asserted, to conclusively address this issue: 'Exchange of population,' Hanumanthaiya said, 'is taking place of its own accord. It is therefore that we have to take it up on the official level and frame our policy accordingly.' He suggested a 'peaceful transfer of population'. Hanumanthaiya was also forceful about this stand on false pretensions when it came to the plight of the Hindus of East Bengal. Speaking of Pakistan's treatment of its minorities, Hanumanthaiya argued that,

> So long as there is peace in Pakistan, I would not suggest exchange of population. If by any chance Pakistan forces the minorities out of Pakistan, I would urge upon the Government of India to take that question on the very same plane and do it more humanly. This idea may look ludicrous but that is the only solution. We must not hesitate to send those Muslim League people to Pakistan who were responsible for its establishment and consequent disorder and suffering. Sure, they will be more at home there.... Even Mahatma Gandhi was not able to succeed in preventing the mass migration from Pakistan to India and from India to Pakistan. Where Mahatma Gandhi failed if others claim to succeed, I can only say 'I will wait and see.' Therefore, if Pakistan periodically follows a policy of ousting the minorities from Pakistan and that is their planned policy so that ultimately it may be a complete Islamic State, we cannot afford to keep quiet. To plead that there is no solution is bankruptcy of statesmanship.

Hanumanthaiya argued that the vacillation was proving to be costly, and some concrete steps were urgently needed to allay the fears of the people across the country.

Nehru's reply to this was rude. He called it an 'approach completely lacking in intelligent thought'. Nehru went on: 'I was amazed that anyone should talk such utter nonsense as he did, in this matter.' Earlier, during the same debate, he was emphatic when he said,

Some people talk vaguely about exchange of populations and all that and we, have to consider every possible aspect of this problem. Now, exchange of populations is something which we have opposed all along. It is something which I consider completely, not only undesirable, but not feasible.

Strange that when he pressed for a complete exchange of population in Punjab, Nehru did not find the proposition 'utter nonsense' or 'vague' because it originated from himself. But when it came to Bengali Hindus of East Bengal, he put a brake on any such proposal.

The Congress's opposition to the CAA today is similar to its spraying a 'saline water douche' on the wounded and bleeding hearts of these displaced persons whose status the CAA aimed to redress permanently. Meanwhile, in West Bengal, the anti-CAA brigade was led by the ruling Trinamool Congress, the communist parties, the Popular Front of India (PFI), and Siddiqullah Chowdhury, a minister in Mamata Banerjee's cabinet and president of the Jamiat-Ulemaa e-Hind's West Bengal chapter. Chowdhury had also contested the 2014 parliamentary elections on a ticket from the All India United Democratic Front (AIUDF), a party led by the Islamist Badruddin Ajmal, whose political base is primarily derived from infiltrators from Bangladesh. All these parties continue to resort to dangerously divisive politics; they obfuscate the historical reason for which Dr Syama Prasad Mookerjee and some of the leading lights of that period had exerted themselves to save a portion of Bengal. By opposing CAA, they are not only negating that reality but are also opposing the Bengali Hindu refugees' legitimate right to treat West Bengal as their home.

As for the Congress, its present leaders have no use for or no memory of the likes of Pandit Maitra, K. Hanumanthaiya, or Dr B.C. Roy. For them, serfdom to a family is the summit of their ambition and the vision of India as a civilizational homeland and motherland can therefore be jettisoned!

The Nehru–Liaquat Pact of 1950 failed to protect the minorities in East Pakistan, and this was compounded by Nehru's peculiar and irrational refusal to effectuate a total exchange of population on the eastern front. He was determined that refugees flowing in from East Pakistan would be provided only with relief and not rehabilitation and would have to go back.

Dr Syama Prasad Mookerjee, speaking in Parliament on 7 August 1950, four months after the Nehru–Liaquat pact had been inked, pointed out how it had failed. It had failed to prevent atrocities and attacks on minorities in East Pakistan. These continuing attacks, desecrations, and killings had shown, Dr Mookerjee told the House, that the 'entire social and economic structure in which Hindus lived has collapsed and it is impossible for them to live there' (1950).

So insensitive was Nehru that he refused to even consider the plight of the Bengali Hindus of East Bengal, even when they pleaded with him in person; at the Jaipur session of the All India Congress Committee (AICC) in 1948, a delegation of Bengali Hindu refugees belonging to the Nikhil Vanga Bastuhara Karam Parishad (NVBKP) led by Gandhians and Congress leaders of East Bengal— among them the veteran Congressmen and Gandhians, Amritlal Chatterjee, Mahadev Bhattacharya, and Nagen Das, all of whom had to come away from East Pakistan and take shelter in West Bengal—called on Nehru to submit a deputation requesting the central government to provide for the rehabilitation of refugees who had come from East Pakistan to West Bengal. They were stunned by the Prime Minister's reaction. Nehru told them, point blank, that 'the refugees were all foreigners' and that the 'Karam Parishad representatives better talk to the Foreign Bureau of the AICC'. Nehru had decided to look upon the refugees from East Bengal as foreigners—people who till the other day carried the Congress flag, fought for India's freedom under Mahatma Gandhi's leadership and were some of the faithful carriers of the Congress's ideology and political programmes.

A year after he had this shocking encounter with Nehru, veteran Congressman Amritlal Chatterjee, addressing a refugee convention in north Kolkata on 30 October 1949, lamented how mother Bengal and mother India were vivisected, and how the Bengali and the Sikh had become foreigner Pakistanis with their religion, culture, education, values, and their womenfolk in danger and profaned. Chatterjee said that under the pressure of circumstances, the government of India was compelled to evacuate the Hindus and Sikhs of West Punjab, but when it came to the Hindus of East Pakistan, it did not make such an effort. Not only did it not undertake such an effort, it refused to even accept that there was a problem. It tried to belittle or minimize the magnitude of the problem.

This attitude of the Congress leadership left a huge historic challenge unaddressed. Despite assuring these hapless people of protection and shelter, the Congress and Nehru turned their backs on them once the partition was done and the pogrom against the minorities began. While Dr Ambedkar, in his seminal book *Pakistan or the Partition of India*, had advocated a complete exchange of population, arguing that the 'transfer of minorities is the only lasting remedy for communal peace is beyond doubt', Mahatma Gandhi is on record as having said on 16 July 1947 after his customary post-prayer meeting address:

> There is the problem of those Hindus who for fear imaginary or real, will have to leave their own homes in Pakistan. If hindrances are created in their daily work or movement or if they are treated as foreigners in their own land, then they will not be able to stay there. In that case the duty of the adjoining province on this side of the border will be to accept them with both arms and to extend to them all legitimate opportunities. They should be made to feel that they have not come to an alien land.

The CAA spoke of this past historic neglect and argued for the need to accept these people with both arms, to extend to them all legitimate opportunities and to make them feel that they have not come to an alien land. But ironically, the Congress then and the Congress now continued to oppose this move. Nehru too, as we have seen, had promised these people that they would be protected and looked after if the need ever arose. He had said, 'Our duty to those who will be in peril in East Bengal, will be to protect them in their own country and to give them shelter in our own country if there is no other way and the situation so demands.'

But Nehru never made any serious move to fulfil or to stand by this promise. In fact, his attitude towards the sufferings and displacement of the Bengali Hindu refugees was expressed in outbursts, 'We discouraged in every possible way the migration of large numbers from one Bengal to the other. Unfortunately, in spite of our discouragement, many came over in hundreds of thousands.'

Nehru harboured a deep animus for Bengali Hindus. Historian of partition and refugees the late A.J. Kamra put it bluntly that Nehru was one of those leaders who had asked the minorities to stay put in East Pakistan in 1947, but soon after Sardar Patel's death, he 'completely betrayed the helpless minorities':

> [There is] no doubt that Pandit Nehru too was the architect of the genocides of the minorities in East Pakistan till the very end of his life in 1964. He tried his utmost to ignore, minimise and brush under the carpet the sufferings of the Hindus and Buddhists of East Pakistan. When millions of Hindus were squeezed out of East Pakistan in 1949–1950, Sardar Patel asked Pakistan for territory in East Pakistan to settle the Hindus. Soon after the death of Sardar Patel in 1950, Pandit Nehru completely betrayed the Hindus and Buddhists of East Pakistan. (2000)

In the 1950s, Nehru began shutting every door to Hindu refugees. 'When the Chief Minister of Bengal, Dr B.C. Roy pleaded with Nehru to open the doors to the wretched refugees, Nehru refused saying, "If we open the door, we will all sink".'

His political heirs today have actively opposed the conferring of citizenship on minorities persecuted and evicted from India's neighbourhood. Nehru's heirs whipped up emotions and attempted to generate a communal frenzy through a deliberate misinterpretation of the Act. In doing this, they displayed a colossal ignorance of partition history and a stony and disdainful indifference to the plight of the refugees who, for seven decades, have been living a near-invisible existence.

Enacting the CAA was a civilizational move; it was the fulfilment of a historic promise and the rectification of a historical wrong. It is a move that will further concretize the vision of a new India; it announces the start of a new phase, a phase in which those long-suffering and ignored will, at last, find a place of dignity and will contribute their energies to this vision of a New India. Those who have opposed it today are the ones who have habitually sided with separatism, forces of disintegration, and elements that wish to see India's march retarded and held captive to the old narrative of fear and division. The real India is rejecting them and will eventually reject them entirely and comprehensively.

3

Congress's Doublespeak on and Neglect of Refugees from East Bengal

We are living in extremely paradoxical times. Savour here one example. Having fanned the fires of violent protests against the Citizenship Amendment Act (CAA) introduced and effectuated by Prime Minister Modi's government and passed by both Houses of Parliament and assented to by the President of India and having given calls to a certain denominational section—namely the Indian Muslims—to hit the streets against CAA, to consider it their right to violently protest, to consider the protests as their ultimate struggle for survival, the Congress party's leaders in Parliament eventually admitted that CAA was not about taking away anyone's citizenship! The party remains leaderless and rudderless and is evolving into a dangerously confused political entity.

That acerbic lawyer of the Congress, the one who was at the forefront of opposing the building of a Ram Temple at Ayodhya, Kapil Sibal, admitted as much in the Rajya Sabha in early March 2020 during the debate on the Delhi violence. Sibal said that it was 'not his contention that CAA will take away citizenship'. That is exactly what Prime Minister Modi, the Union Home Minister Amit Shah, and the entire phalanx of the BJP had been saying since the night when the CAA was passed in Parliament. The CAA was meant to confer citizenship and legitimize and dignify the existence of those lakhs of people who were evicted from the land and home of their ancestors due to targeted and systematic religious persecution. These persecutions were the effects and after-effects of Partition and could not be ignored.

The Pakistan state's Islamic character led to this behaviour towards its minorities ever since it was carved out of India. The dilemma and plight of the minorities of Pakistan, especially on its eastern flank, then known as East Bengal and later as East Pakistan till the formation of Bangladesh in 1971, was, among others, best described in Jawaharlal Nehru's words when he said sometime in early 1949 that 'the basic difficulty of the situation is that the policy of religious and communal state followed by the Pakistan Government inevitably produces a sense of lack of full citizenship and a continuous insecurity among those who do not belong to the majority community'. Surely the Congress will have no dispute with Nehru's words and description of the situation, provided the Congress of today has a sense of their own party's history and past.

Ever since its formation, the leadership of Pakistan pressed to declare it as an Islamic state. In this Islamic state, non-Muslims would live as second-class and persecuted citizens. Despite professions to the contrary, minorities, especially Hindus in Pakistan, received a raw deal. The *Amrita Bazar Patrika*, one of the most reliable documenters and chroniclers of the eastern partition, referring to the conditions of the Hindus in East Bengal, wrote thus:

They have no share in the executive: 25 per cent of the people have no representative in the Cabinet or in the all-powerful bureaucracy. They have no share in legislation, for brute majority counts and the voice of the minority is but a cry in the wilderness. They have no share in the judiciary: a community which has produced jurists and judges of international reputation for a century or more cannot provide even a Munsif for East Pakistan Judicial Service.

Pravash Chandra Lahiry, a former minister in East Pakistan and freedom fighter, best described the status of non-Muslims, the minorities in Pakistan:

Monolithic unity in a homogenous state was the aim of the leaders of Pakistan and they spared no pains to achieve it at all costs, even at the expense of eliminating the undesirable segregated minority from the national life of Pakistan by a planned process of visible and invisible oppressions and persecutions. The logic of the situation is such that in such a hostile atmosphere and uncongenial environment, surcharged with intense racial and communal hatred, a minority community by virtue of their religion only, who have been economically crippled, socially disorganised and politically impotent without any opportunity and freedom for self-development and self-expression, can hardly exist, nay survive as an active element in the country. (1964)

As a consequence of these policies, the minorities, Lahiry noted, have 'become completely demoralised and have lost the vitality of resisting the onslaughts of the rulers on their education, culture, spirit and patriotism. They are suffering from a colossal sense of defeatism' (ibid.). To add to their psychological sense of defeatism, Lahiry lamented, having had a bitter experience of fourteen years in East Pakistan, 'The Muslim leaders of Pakistan have systematically manifested their supposed superiority in all walks of life through their aggressive nationalism.'

By opposing the CAA, the Congress was, in effect, repudiating this historic past. It was blinding itself to the plight of the Hindus in Pakistan and was trying to negate its own past.

The first round of pogrom began in 1950—Hindus in droves were compelled to leave their home and hearth in East Bengal and move to the pavements of West Bengal. All the while, the Pakistani government claimed that they did so out of their free will and that there was peace as far as the minorities were concerned. It was Raj Kumar Chakravarty, a doughty freedom fighter and member of the Pakistan Constituent Assembly, who countered this lie. Chakravarty told the Pakistan Constituent Assembly:

> Certainly, the people are not leaving their homes and hearths, the land of their forefathers where they have lived for generations, for the mere fun of it … the fact is that there is a sense of insecurity in the minds of the people of the minority community. There is a want of confidence in the government of Eastern Pakistan…. I say with all sense of responsibility that I possess that there is no doubt peace but it is the peace of the grave that exists with regard to the minority communities in East Bengal.

Bhupendra Kumar Dutta, Raj Kumar Chakravarty's colleague in the Pakistan Constituent Assembly, himself a widely revered revolutionary and icon among the young revolutionaries of Bengal, speaking in the Constituent Assembly echoed

Chakravarty. Dutta spoke of how the February pogroms came as a rude shock to the minorities of Pakistan:

> The recent happenings have given a rude shock to the sense of security of the minority community. Whatever the sources of inspiration, the minorities see that it is people belonging to the overwhelming majority that attacked them without the remotest provocation on their part … and people cannot live every moment fearing what the next may bring.

Both Chakravarty and Dutta were Congressmen.

Speaking in the Pakistan Constituent Assembly in 1952, Dutta again spoke of the minorities who were being continuously excluded from all professions and walks of life in East Bengal. Even in 1952, the process was continuing unabated. I quote these in some detail in order to emphasize the continuous saga of persecution and exclusion faced by the minorities of Pakistan. Often narrated by Congressmen and freedom fighters themselves, Dutta argued that:

> Some of our minority representatives often say that the worst problem for the minorities in Pakistan is educational. That problem is doubtless there. But to me the basic problem is that of livelihood. Practically all sources of livelihood have been and are being closed to them. Government jobs, jobs in private firms, they are not to have. In the professions there has been a silent campaign of boycott, often encouraged by officials and non-officials. Control shops, licences for motor buses and taxis the Hindus have very quickly been deprived of. Formerly, some of them had agencies for the various oil companies, The Imperial Tobacco Co., the I.C.I. and such other firms. They have almost all changed hands.

If they are some professors or school masters, as soon as a fresh graduate is available to replace an experienced M.A., some fault is found with the latter, in the long run he would be accused of anti-State propensities. If he does not get into other troubles, he must, at least, give up his job and run for safety across the border. This has happened even to many village postmasters. Even the poorer folk, the peasant, the fisherman prove no exceptions.

Dutta complained how when anything happens, 'any agitation by the majority community, any quarrel between Pakistan and India the Hindus are given out as working against the security and integrity of Pakistan as the agents of India'. This was 'most exasperating', and as days passed, the Hindus were

> more and more depressed, although we won our freedom five years back. We feel no heart in our work, as we know we feel, the majority fixed by birth is wholly callous to the voice of reason and justice and humanity, although that majority would call it an Islamic State. The prevailing attitude appears to be, they lose nothing if the minority suffers or in despair leaves.

His pleas fell on deaf ears in Pakistan, and the Congress in India continued to be equally deaf to their plight.

Dhirendra Nath Dutta, another distinguished Hindu member of the Pakistan Constituent Assembly, was also a freedom fighter and once a close associate of C.R. Das, a Bengali nationalist who would be eventually killed by the Pakistan army in 1971, starkly and best described the dilemma and agony of the Hindus in Pakistan. 'There is a great deal of mistrust,' he said, 'If you put on *loongi*, poor

Muslim clothes in East Bengal, it is said that we disguise ourselves. If we put on dhoti, then it is said that we have come from West Bengal. There is such a sense of mistrust and this has been engineered under the Government of Pakistan.'

The Hazratbal relics theft in 1963–64 generated a reaction against Hindus in East Pakistan, leading to massive anti-Hindu pogroms in Dhaka in January 1964. Trailokya Nath Chakravarty, an iconic freedom fighter of the Anushilan Samiti, who spent years in the Cellular Jail, then 75 years old, described the plight of the Hindus in Dhaka. Chakravarty lived in East Bengal and despite his iconic status as a freedom fighter and his popularity among all sections, he chose to stay in a refugee camp of more than 7,000 Hindus during those difficult days. His letter of 19 March 1964 gives an idea of the plight of minorities in East Pakistan even seventeen years after partition. Surely the Congress and its leaders knew of their condition. A freedom fighter's testimony must surely be counted as authentic:

> What an irony of Fate? We are citizens of this State but cannot move about freely, are confined in a cage and friends of the other community come to see us in this cage. Members of the other community can walk the streets freely, have opened stalls on the [relief] camp compound and are hawking goods there, I don't have that freedom, why not? What crime have I committed? What has happened this time is not rioting which can occur only between two contending parties, but one-sided attack, looting and killing. One side attacks and the other flees in fear of life. Those who have been victims of looting or have been killed ask 'What crime have we committed since we do not dabble

in politics, do not meddle with the activities of the people of other community, do not quarrel with our neighbours, are citizens of this country, share its prosperity, sorrow or happiness, pay Government rent regularly, are loyal subjects; then why should we be killed, why our houses should be looted or burnt, our children killed before our very eyes, our womenfolk dishonoured? Is there no remedy for it? Are we responsible for what is happening in some other country? When innocent people are killed on railway trains, buses and steam launches, why members of the other community merely look on like silent onlookers? Why do they not stop the wrong-doers? Is not their inaction an indication of their tacit consent? If communal riots occur 17 years after Independence, then who can guarantee that these will not occur in the future? Migration means immense suffering and even death for many Hindus, why then do they want to leave their hearth and home and property?' Lack of security is perhaps the only reason.

The Enquiry Committee set up by the Indian Commission of Jurists in 1965 on the 'Recurrent Exodus of Minorities from East Pakistan and Disturbances in India' spoke of the 'recent large-scale exodus of minority communities which include not only Hindus but Christians and Buddhists from East Pakistan'. Detailing the process of denuding Pakistan of its minorities that had started since partition and continued, the Enquiry Committee recorded how:

A large-scale requisitioning of Hindu houses and properties took place. The educational institutions were largely manned by Hindus and practically all the schools were run by Hindus. There was a squeeze of the teachers and professors in order to make room for Muslims. Hindu students were forced to leave the hostels. Thus, attempts were made to dislodge the Hindus from their dominant position. This discrimination, unfortunately, went right down the scale to the petty shop keeper and the small land holder. The result was that even those who had stayed behind with the intention of making East Pakistan their home, because they were born and brought up in that area, began to feel that life would be very difficult for them and the migration continued.

The Nehru dispensation never attempted to address this sense of insecurity among the minorities of Pakistan. The questions therefore that beg attention and answers is why the Congress, if it has finally admitted that CAA is not meant to snatch away citizenship but to confer it, then persisted for three months in fanning passions and violence, in inciting a section of the population, in insisting in states in which it is in power that its government pass anti-CAA resolutions and thus challenge our democratic and Constitutional fabric and essence? Why did it persist in inciting a revolt against our Parliamentary structure? Why did it spite the plight of Hindu refugees, why did it refuse to accept that a life of dignity is what they deserve, why did it vociferously resist the passing of CAA and ask people to take to the streets, why did it seem to side with anti-India fronts like the Popular Front of India (PFI) and work to destabilize India internally and internationally? These are questions that posterity will definitely ask of the Congress.

Dr B.C. Roy, one of the tallest leaders of the Congress from West Bengal and its chief minister during those crucial years and decades, had a mind of his own and supported the demand for the creation of West Bengal. Dr Roy lamented in a press conference in Kolkata, on 20 March 1951, that the 'refugees have a great grievance, a very natural one, indeed against everybody in West Bengal and in India, even perhaps against Providence, because they have been uprooted, put to shame and difficulties for no fault of theirs'. A few days before this, speaking in the West Bengal Legislative Assembly, Dr Roy had candidly admitted that 'neither he nor the Central Government had an idea of the nature of the influx and of the number of the migrants'. He pointed out how the Union Government led by Jawaharlal Nehru was fixated on the notion that the migrants from East Bengal/East Pakistan 'would return to their homes as soon as the situation improved in East Pakistan'.

To a question in Parliament, Nehru had stated that his 'Government was aware that a considerable number of Hindus had migrated from East to West Bengal. But migrations were not desirable and should not be encouraged, as they would bring a great deal of suffering in their train'. Nehru argued that the 'conditions would improve so as to enable the minorities in East Bengal to resume their normal lives and vocations. He however admitted that refugees coming from East Pakistan were being harassed in various ways on their way'.

In a letter to Dr B.C. Roy in August 1948, Nehru called for trying to prevent the influx of refugees from East Bengal into India. 'I have been terribly anxious throughout,' he wrote to Dr Roy, 'to prevent this, whatever might happen. I still think that every effort should be made to prevent it. I think that it was a very wrong thing for some of the Hindu leaders of East Bengal to come to West Bengal.' This was typical of Jawaharlal Nehru. He refused to acknowledge the cause of this migration and displacement and take it up forcefully with the Pakistan establishment. Driven by a false sense of prestige, he wanted to either prevent the Bengali Hindus from coming to India in order to save themselves or force them to return to the communal cauldron of East Bengal if they had already come to India. In order to ensure that they were compelled to return, he decided to starve and corner them; his policy was to desist from providing them with rehabilitation. This was, as we shall see later, in sharp contrast to his approach on the Punjab front, where he not only advocated a complete exchange of population but also arranged for relief and rehabilitation.

Nehru's government insisted that Bengali Hindu refugees from East Pakistan would only be provided with relief and not rehabilitation. Despite realizing that his *entente cordiale* with Liaquat was failing and his pact was falling apart and more and more minorities were being driven out of Pakistan, Nehru turned a blind eye to the plight of the Bengali Hindu refugees. We shall see later the detailed expose of the failure of the Nehru–Liaquat Pact that Dr Mookerjee made on various occasions. It would suffice for the time being to mention his famous intervention in Parliament on 7 August 1950. Dr Mookerjee asked a few fundamental questions that revealed that the much-touted Pact was failing on the ground. Syama Prasad asked:

> What was the main purpose of the Pact? Was not the chief object of the pact that Hindus would be able to live in East Bengal with a sense of security and without fear; that there would be no exodus and those who had come away would gradually of their own accord feel emboldened to go back to their home? Was it not the purpose of the Pact that there would be a sense of security in the minds of the minorities

themselves so that they could decide on their own course of action without any fear or expectation of favour from any quarter? Judged from this standpoint the Pact has failed. The exodus continues; the intense sense of insecurity in the minds of the minority continues.

Was it because he was determined to prove the success of his failing pact that Nehru was hell-bent on ensuring that the Bengali Hindu refugees from East Bengal must all go back? These are historical facts that the present Congress has no idea of. It opposed CAA and attempted to cancel its narrative only because it is opposed to Narendra Modi and has always refused to side with the interests of Hindus.

Nehru's Relief and Rehabilitation Minister Mohanlal Saxena, to a categorical question by none other than Dr Meghnad Saha, spilt out the matter when he said that the refugees 'would not be given rehabilitation. They would get temporary shelter in relief camps'. Saxena had also instructed the West Bengal government to set up refugee camps near the border. Perhaps he was hoping that as soon as peace was restored, the refugees would go back to their homes in East Pakistan. Saxena told Dr Saha, 'Those who had left East Bengal for fear of their lives would soon return to their homes as soon as peace was restored. The question of rehabilitation therefore did not arise.' Since the 'influx had come with the suddenness of a summer storm and no one had any idea as yet of its ravages. So, there could be no plan for rehabilitation at the moment.'

To Dr Saha, it was clear that Nehru's government did not want to take responsibility for these beleaguered and battered Bengali Hindus. He reminded Saxena of 'the pledges given to the Hindus of East and West Pakistan by the national leaders. They could not now simply shrug off the burden of the East Bengal refugees. That would amount to a breach of promise repeatedly given to them by Gandhi, Jawaharlal Nehru and other leaders'. Saxena's brief was simply to communicate to the leaders of eastern India that the 'Central Government's commitment to the East Bengal refugees was relief and not rehabilitation'.

A letter to Nehru's rehabilitation minister best summed up the Nehruvian approach to the Bengali Hindu refugees. 'If you could chalk out a scheme of planned exodus from Sind,' the letter writer asked:

> What makes you fight shy of planning a similar scheme for the East Bengal Hindus, is an enigma to a common man. The East Bengal Hindus fought as much as anybody else, if not more, in the cause of India's freedom, and anybody with a head on his shoulders should understand that they are entitled to make their own choice in the matter of rehabilitation. If the play of some inscrutable political factors has placed them under the Pakistan Government, you cannot make a capital out of it by torpedoing their rights of citizenship in the Indian Union.

Historian Prafulla Chakrabarti, whose seminal work on refugees we have discussed, precisely describes the Nehru government's attitude towards the Bengali Hindu refugees from East Bengal. Chakrabarti writes,

> [Nehru] did not pause to consider that its policy towards the West Pakistan refugees was completely different from what it now proposed to pursue towards the East Bengal refugees. In the case of Punjab, the Central Government easily accepted exchange of population and property. Even when the riots were over there was no proposal of a status

quo ante. On the contrary the problem of rehabilitation was sought to be solved with the outmost expedition. But in the case of East Bengal refugees Nehru could never accept the idea of an exchange of population between East and West Bengal. Yet no one knew better that the basis of partition was religion and that Pakistan had deliberately chosen to be an Islamic State where there could be no equal status for non-Muslims. (1999)

Dr B.C. Roy pointed out how only later did Nehru realize that what the refugees from East Bengal/East Pakistan needed was both 'relief and rehabilitation, and rehabilitation meant not only a plot of land and a house but gainful occupation and recovery from the low psychic state produced by uprooting'. Even after this, little was done in terms of rehabilitation for these refugees.

The fashionable protestors in Lutyens Delhi and stone-pelters of Jamia would hardly know the agonies of these refugees. In the context of West Bengal, it is also doubly ironic that the Congress leaders from the state, especially the party's then floor leader in Lok Sabha, Adhir Chowdhury, just to keep his infiltrator vote bank intact in Murshidabad, ignored the history of his own party's leaders in the past and opposed CAA. Had he known his party's past, Chowdhury would have at least entered into a civil debate on the issue.

At the time of Independence, the refugees were promised protection in their countries and shelter and equal rights in India if they ever left their countries because of religious persecution and discrimination. These promises were made by many leaders, and after Independence, a number of other leaders continued to speak for their rights and continued to highlight their plight, but hardly ever did they attempt to settle the issue once and for all.

Interestingly, it will be relevant to mention in this context, that on 16 August 1966, veteran Jana Sangh leader Niranjan Varma, then Member of Rajya Sabha, asked three pointed questions to the then Union External Affairs Minister Sardar Swaran Singh. These questions were:

- What is the present position of the Nehru–Liaquat Pact, which was concluded in 1950 after the last India–Pakistan conflict?
- Are both countries still acting according to the terms of the Pact?
- Since what year has Pakistan been violating the Pact?

To Verma's first question, Swaran Singh said, 'The Nehru–Liaquat Pact of 1950 is a standing agreement between India and Pakistan. It requires each country to ensure that its minorities enjoy complete equality of citizenship with others and receive treatment identical to that available for other nationals of their country.' Singh's answer to the second question was that 'though in India, the rights and security of the minorities have been continuously and effectively safeguarded, Pakistan has persistently contravened the provisions of the Pact through consistent neglect and harassment of the members of the minority community'. Swaran Singh's answer to the third question is more crucial for us since it points to the failure of the Nehru–Liaquat pact. Singh replied that 'instances of such violations started coming to notice almost immediately after the inception of the Pact'.

Sixteen years ago, Dr Syama Prasad Mookerjee had exposed the immediate failure of the Pact that Swaran

Singh, as the Foreign Minister accepted much later. One of the basic arguments for the CAA spoke of the failure of this Pact and of the trail of agony and suffering that it had led to for the Hindus of Pakistan. The Congress of today deliberately chose to ignore and obfuscate that truth. Its stand was a deliberate insult to the memories of those valiant Hindu leaders who fought and struggled for the rights of minorities in Pakistan.

4

Dalits and the Demand for a Bengali Hindu Homeland and Their Persecution in Islamic Pakistan

It was unclear what drove parties such as the Bahujan Samaj Party (BSP) to oppose the passage of the CAA. Had the BSP leadership, which had supported the abrogation of Article 370 on the grounds that it would provide for reservation to the marginalized sections in the region, read up on the history of India's partition in some detail, especially how partition had affected the Dalits of East Pakistan, it would have perhaps had a rethink. Most of the persecuted minorities of these countries in India's neighbourhood are Dalits; the persecution of the Namasudras—the valiant Matuas in East Pakistan and later Bangladesh—is one of the most disturbing episodes of our recent history.

The present crop of BSP leaders would perhaps not know that their founding icon Kanshiram had been vocal on the Marichjhapi issue where a violent eviction and massacre of Dalit Hindu refugees was ordered by West Bengal's first communist government. The Marichjhapi refugees appealed to Kanshiram's All India Backward and Minority Communities Employees Federation (BAMCEF) for support against the murderous assault of Jyoti Basu's communist government. Having been formed just a year earlier, BMACEF had not yet acquired the political and social clout its political front, the BSP, would have in the years to come. Kanshiram lamented the condition of the Dalit refugees and the treatment meted out to them:

Immediately after the exit of the British in 1947, there was a sharp and steep slump in the Namasudra Movement. The partition of India ruined many a people, but those harmed maximum were the Namasudra. Not only the people and the community were ruined, but also their movement was completely destroyed. Today the Namasudra are the rootless people. Divided in two countries, their roots are in Bangladesh and branches in India. Bangladesh government is always eager to uproot them, whereas the government of India and West Bengal are ever angry and hostile. The massacre of Marichjhapi and the sad plight of those in Dandakaranya, Andaman, Nicobar and elsewhere tell its own tale. After all this if they are expecting some help or sympathy from the High Caste Hindus, they are hoping against hope.

Complaining about the negative attitude of the CPI(M) government towards the Dalits and their non-inclusion in the West Bengal cabinet, Kanshiram complained,

Unfortunately the CPI(M) Government was unable to see ability in them. They say, they do not believe in caste considerations, they include people in the cabinet on the basis of their ability. And on this consideration, they had not included any Scheduled Caste (SC) in the Cabinet of West Bengal. But the Scheduled Caste people still cling to CPI(M), perhaps they are helpless and [have] nowhere to go.

The BSP today is not the one which Kanshiram had founded. It has allowed itself to be held hostage to the politics of appeasement and vote bank. The question that parties like the BSP would have to answer for posterity when historically evaluated is how the BSP leadership did not support the CAA which would, in fact, provide a life of dignity and certainty to a large number of refugees who were from the marginalized communities? How was it that a political entity like the BSP which had once built up an entire political ecosystem professing to work for the empowerment of Dalits oppose the CAA?

As a sample for those self-professed Dalit, communist and Congress leaders who opposed the CAA, Sukumar Biswas and Hiroshi Sato, in their *Religion and Politics in Bangladesh and West Bengal: A Study of Communal Relations* document how in January 1950 (the period when the attacks on minorities in East Pakistan intensified) a pogrom was unleashed on tribals—Santals—by the East Pakistan police:

> Village after village was indiscriminately burnt down, peasants were beaten and tortured mercilessly. They created a reign of terror by free looting, and raping of the Santal women went at will. 24 Santal peasants succumbed to death due to police torture.... Innumerable Santals were killed in Nawabganj and Rajshahi Jails.... The pervasive and multi-directional torturing compelled several Santal peasants to emigrate to West Bengal.

These Santals were active participants in the historic Tebhaga movement led by communist party leaders in East Pakistan! Yet, both Mayawati and Sitaram Yechury have opposed the CAA. They do not want Scheduled Tribes (STs) and SCs, among others, who came away to India due to religious persecution to be conferred with Indian citizenship!

Plenty of records and documentation exist on how people from these sections of society were driven away, along with others, from East Pakistan. The *Amrita Bazar Patrika* reported on 6 March 1950, for instance:

> After a month since the atrocities had been committed on the Santals, disturbances again started on February 28 last. Since then, hundreds, of Hindus of all classes began to cross the border into Maldah district in the Indian Union. During their journey these people have been subjected to all sorts of harassment; their womenfolk especially suffered great indignities.... The Ansars are snatching away whatever these unfortunate people have with them. A month back nearly 800 Santals fled away from Nachole Police Station.... In Singhrill village one Rahim Bux occupied a house belonging to the leader of the Mahato community of the village. Thus, people of the village became very much panicky. As a result of this widespread Hindu baiting, Hindus of all classes began to leave those areas for India.

The *Amrita Bazar Patrika* issue of 23 March 1950 reported how the Pakistan armed forces and Ansars, on the point of rifles, 'drove away 20 families [Santals] of village Hariharpur, adjacent to Balurghat, and broke open the roofs of the houses and took away huge quantities of C.I. sheets, paddy, rice, mustard seeds, jute and utensils'.

The undeclared objective of the Pakistan state was the complete political disenfranchisement of the Dalits and then to hold on to some as hostages and drive out the rest. One of the objectives of the February 1950 pogroms against Hindus in East Pakistan, was, argued Samar Guha—a veteran freedom fighter and parliamentarian and one of the staunchest voices for the persecuted refugees of East Bengal—to push to the other side of the border, 'militant Scheduled Caste and tribal people, living in compact masses and constituting local majority in frontier zones of East Bengal adjoining the Indian Union'.

Having unleashed the pogrom, Guha argued, the Pakistan establishment ensured that the remaining backward-class Hindus, who constituted the 'major bulk of the non-Muslim population', once the first few rounds of displacement had occurred, would pose no more 'hindrance to [the] Islamic indoctrination of [the] Eastern wing of Pakistan'. By distributing some 'petty privileges to some selected people of the present backward classes among non-Muslim communities', the Pak establishment 'expect[ed] to keep them in a state of subservience and easily manageable within the vortex of Muslim influence'. By 1950, the minorities in East Bengal predominantly consisted of the backward caste. They were demoralized, and thus, Guha pointed out, for the Muslim League government of Pakistan 'constituted no problem'. Since the Scheduled Caste and the other backward classes were the 'main bulk of the minority' living in Pakistan, the Pak establishment wanted to control them for various political reasons. In Guha's opinion, this control 'particularly was stopping migration of Indian Mussulmans to Pakistan and also for keeping them as "hostage" for their security'.

The anti-Hindu February 1950 pogroms drove Dalits in large numbers to India. In the second wave of migration between 1950 and 1957, with 2.1 million people moving from East to West Bengal, intelligence reports indicated 'that about 95% refugees' were Namasudras. The Dalits were given a raw deal in Pakistan and their leaders, namely Jogendra Nath Mandal of the AISCF and Pakistan's first law and labour minister, who had championed the cause of a Dalit–Muslim League coalition and had opposed the division of Bengal and the creation of West Bengal, had to resign and flee to India in 1950. While we shall briefly look at Mandal's 8,000-word resignation letter which remains a testimony to the oppression and atrocities committed on Dalits by the Pak Muslim League government, we must also look at those Dalit leaders who had warned Dalits against remaining in a Muslim Pakistan and urged them to migrate to India and had vocally and actively supported Dr Syama Prasad Mookerjee's demand for the creation of a Hindu majority West Bengal as part of the union of India.

Let us start with Babasaheb Dr B.R. Ambedkar. Soon after partition and independence, disturbed by the scale of violence and attacks, Dr Ambedkar issued a statement denouncing the Pakistan Government. He complained that the Scheduled Castes were not allowed to come to Hindustan and that they were being forcibly converted to Islam. He also complained that in the Hyderabad State under the Nizam, Scheduled Castes were being 'forcibly converted to Islam in order to increase the strength of the Muslim'. Dhananjay Keer, one of his earliest biographers, records that by November 1947, Dr Ambedkar publicly advised his people in Pakistan to move to India:

> I would like to tell the Scheduled Castes who happen today to be impounded inside Pakistan to come over to India by such means as may be available to them. The second thing I want to say is that it would be fatal for the Scheduled Castes, whether in Pakistan or in Hyderabad, to put their faith in Muslims or the Muslim League. It has become a habit with the Scheduled Castes to look upon the Muslims as their friends simply because they dislike the Hindus. This is a mistaken view. (*Free Press Journal*, 28 November 1947). (2016)

Dr Ambedkar also appealed to the Scheduled Castes in Pakistan and Hyderabad 'not to succumb to conversion to Islam as an easy way of escape; and to all those who were forcibly converted to Islam, he pledged his word that he would see that they were received back into the fold and treated as brethren'. To Nehru, Dr Ambedkar appealed to 'take speedy steps in evacuating the Scheduled Castes from Pakistan'.

Throughout 1946 and early 1947, Jogendra Nath Mandal was a vociferous advocate of Pakistan. In March 1947, when Dr Syama Prasad Mookerjee issued a public statement calling for the creation of a Bengali Hindu homeland by carving out a portion of Bengal and preventing the entire province from being included in Pakistan, he was speaking for the Hindus as a whole. The communists and their left-leaning intellectuals and academics have always argued that the ploy to carve out West Bengal was a Hindu upper-caste, 'bhadralok' movement to safeguard their dominance and monopoly. Nothing could be far from the truth. A look at the stand of some of the Dalit leaders of that era makes it clear that apart from J.N. Mandal and some of his acolytes and the Muslim League, the majority of Scheduled Caste leaders, or at least those whose opinions mattered and who had a mass base among their people, supported the call for the creation of a Hindu-majority West Bengal.

In his March 1947 statement, Dr Mookerjee argued that:

> Ten years of communal *raj* [10 years of Muslim League rule] in Bengal, has produced disastrous results in every sphere of life. In respect of education, trade, commerce, services, land and property, women's honour, religious rights, the minority community in Bengal has suffered immeasurably at the hands of a ruthless communal administration. What Bengal has passed through is not a mere communal struggle. It is a sinister and planned attempt on the part of an organised government to utilise its machinery secretly and openly to reduce the minority community to a state of serfdom.

Dr Mookerjee saw the salvation of the Hindu minorities of undivided Bengal in 'demanding for ourselves a separate province which will be large enough in area and population and wherein will reside more than two-thirds of the total Hindu population of Bengal'. How could 45 per cent of Bengal's population be subsumed to a majority which has run a communal government over the last decade? Is it wrong to ask for a separate arrangement in that case? Dr Mookerjee asked:

> If we find that the whole of Bengal is going to be dominated by communal frenzy and 45 per cent of its population reduced to a state of slavery, only because they follow a particular religious faith, is it a crime on our part to demand

that we must have our own territory where we can live as free men, and build up our own culture, our own social and economic life in accordance with our best tradition? I fail to see how by allowing ourselves to remain as slaves under a communal *raj* in a so-called united Bengal, we can advance the cause of nationalism.

To those who said that since 45 per cent constituted a large minority of nearly 21 million people, no government could crush them, Dr Mookerjee's reply was prescient as it was precise:

It is said that 45 per cent of Bengal's population comprising nearly 25 million of people constitute such a large number that no government can possibly crush them. This is nothing but an idle and self-deceiving slogan. The Hyderabad State today includes 90 per cent Hindus but they are groaning under a tyrannical rule which is predominantly communal. It is not the number that matters; what matters is the system of administration under which the people are compelled to live.

In April 1947, at the Hindu Mahasabha's provincial conference at Tarakeshwar, Hooghly, N.C. Chatterjee, president of the Bengal Provincial Hindu Mahasabha, appealed to the delegates to 'declare today that as the Muslim League persists in its fantastic idea of establishing Pakistan in Bengal, the Hindus of Bengal must constitute a separate province under a strong national government'. It is not, Chatterjee asserted, 'a question of partition. This is a question of life and death for us, the Bengalee Hindus'. Chatterjee also mentioned that 'over 60 per cent of the members of the Scheduled Castes [of Bengal] would be in the new province' and that this meant 'that their "economic and civic rights" would be safeguarded'.

Dr Mookerjee reiterated that he conceived of 'no other solution of the communal problem in Bengal than to divide the province and to let the two major communities residing here to live in peace and freedom'. The Tarakeswar conference authorized Dr Mookerjee 'to take all steps for the establishment of a separate homeland for the Hindus of Bengal in collaboration with all the nationalist elements'.

Not many remember today that the West Bengal Congress 'accepted the idea almost immediately' and passed a resolution which argued that those portions of Bengal 'as are desirous of remaining within the Union of India should be allowed to remain so and be formed in a separate province within the Union of India'. A *hartal* in Kolkata in support of partition was followed by a statement issued by 'fifty jurists of the Calcutta High Court' who 'pressed for the partition of Bengal on the ground that by going to Pakistan the Bengali Hindus would only exchange one form of slavery for another, and that they needed a homeland of their own'. On 1 April 1947, 'eleven members of the Constituent Assembly from Bengal submitted a memorandum to the viceroy supporting the partition of the province'.

The Kolkata business establishment led by none other than G.D. Birla expressed 'solid support' to Dr Mookerjee's proposal of partitioning Bengal. The Chamber of Commerce in its meeting on 30 April 1947 supported the partition of Bengal. On 1 June 1947, Dr Mookerjee addressing the Bengali community in Delhi 'called for a division of Bengal on "linguistic, cultural and economic considerations if India had to be divided"'. This shows that a cross-section of public opinion supported the demand for the creation of a Hindu homeland of West Bengal.

Jogendra Nath Mandal went all out to oppose the move. He received support from the Muslim League premier H.S. Suhrawardy. Mandal denounced the demand for the creation of West Bengal and claimed that the 'majority of non-Muslims in Bengal were not behind the demand'. He crisscrossed the province 'lecturing against the proposed Partition' and also tried with the help of local Muslim League functionaries to recruit 'SC volunteers in every district to form an opinion in favour' of the anti-partition campaign he had launched. Perhaps under the influence of Suhrawardy, Mandal also declared that he did 'not visualise Bengal of the future as a province linked with either Pakistan or Hindustan, but as an independent Undivided, Sovereign State'. Dr Mookerjee threw a spanner in this move to detach the whole of Bengal from India. Apart from leading a public movement against the attempt, Dr Mookerjee wrote to Viceroy Mountbatten in March 1947, spelling out the rationale and argument for the creation of West Bengal. On the 'loose talk' of a sovereign undivided Bengal, Dr Mookerjee told Mountbatten:

> We do not understand its significance at all nor do we support it in any way. This will give us, Hindus, no relief whatsoever. Sovereign undivided Bengal will be a virtual Pakistan. Who will frame the constitution of Sovereign Bengal? Obviously, this will be left in the hands of the majority of the Moslem League who will be guided by fanatical notions of a separate nationhood and we are not prepared to trust our fate to them. Further we do not in any case want to be cut off from the rest of India and we are

not prepared to make any compromise on this issue on any consideration whatsoever.

Suhrawardy, meanwhile, worked overtime to debunk the partition proposal and to win over the Scheduled Caste community of Bengal. He assured the SCs:

> With a degree of confidence that in framing the constitution [of Pakistan], the wishes of the Scheduled Castes will be given the utmost consideration, and if they desire separate electorates for the preservation of their political rights and culture, then there is little doubt that their wish will be fulfilled.

But SC leaders who mattered in Bengal did not fall for Suhrawardy's assurances nor for Mandal's arguments. In April 1947, P.R. Thakur, the iconic leader of the Matua community and member of the Constituent Assembly, who had clearly thrown his weight behind the West Bengal proposal took on Mandal. Thakur said that even Dr Ambedkar, Mandal's 'political Guru' did not support Pakistan. In fact, he said, 'What is more, Dr Ambedkar is definitely in favour of Bengal Partition Movement.' Thakur argued that Mandal's views on this 'crucial issue' were at variance 'with the considered opinion not only of the Depressed Classes League but also of the Depressed Classes Federation, two most representative and recognised organisations of the Scheduled Castes people all over India'. Had Mandal any sympathy for the 'wishes and sentiments of the SC people of Bengal', Thakur stated, Mandal 'should have persuaded the Muslim League not to insist on Pakistan in Bengal but to work for a United Bengal under the Indian Union'.

Thakur opposed Pakistan and therefore advocated partition and the formation of West Bengal. He too wanted Bengal to remain united, but unlike Mandal, who wanted a united Bengal as a sovereign and independent state, Thakur wanted Bengal to be part of the Indian Union and was unequivocal in that demand. As early as 19 December 1946, Thakur made a crucial intervention in the Constituent Assembly. He spoke for a large number of SCs when he told the Constituent Assembly that the SCs were 'no doubt a part and parcel of the great Hindu community' and that the Depressed Classes were the

> original inhabitants of this country.... India belongs to us and we cannot tolerate the idea that this ancient mother country of ours will be divided between the Muslims and the Caste Hindus only.... We strongly repudiate any claim of the Muslim League to take away our beloved Bengal and constitute her into Pakistan.... We shall fight tooth and nail to maintain the integrity of India intact.

Thakur also told the Constituent Assembly how the Muslim League in Bengal was 'trying to get support of a section of the Depressed Classes' to try and pave the way for 'their fantastic Pakistan. But, fortunately, this section of the Depressed Classes is very small'. Thakur appealed to the CA to see to it that nothing was done 'in regard to Bengal without the consent of the Depressed Classes' who were in overwhelming numbers. In May 1947, when the movement for the creation of West Bengal moved towards success, Thakur assured his followers in East Bengal that 'they should not be disturbed by the false idea that they would be doomed forever after the partition of Bengal. I can assure them that Hindu-India will pay their first and foremost attention to the solution of their acute problem'. It is said that Thakur had met Mahatma Gandhi, who had assured him that free India would stand by the beleaguered SCs of East Bengal. Dr Syama Prasad Mookerjee, during his extensive and repeated tours of East Bengal while campaigning for Partition in East Bengal villages, also promised to stand with them if they faced adversities as a result of Partition.

While Mandal was on a galloping spree to promote a sovereign and united Bengal, other SC leaders joined Thakur in opposing Mandal. Manorajan Das, secretary of the Noakhali Taposili Hindu Samiti, reminded Mandal of how he had not acted when SCs of Noakhali were attacked after Direct Action when he and 'about 400 men, women and children were attacked, many of them forcibly converted and held captive for twenty-six days'; Mandal, despite being a minister, did nothing, and on the contrary, issued a statement that 'SCs were fine'. Das argued that the SCs had a 'bitter test of a Muslim League government during the recent riots [Noakhali], and so they would wholeheartedly support the division of Bengal to get rid of the Muslim League rule'.

Bejoy Krishna Sarkar, a Scheduled Caste MLA from the Congress, asked Mandal in a press statement what he had done, besides lending support to 'Direct Action', to 'save the lives and properties of innocent SCs who lost everything in Calcutta and Noakhali'. Muslim *goonda*s, Sarkar reminded Mandal, 'made no discrimination between Caste Hindus and the Scheduled Castes'. Birat Mandal from the Scheduled Caste Association 'issued a press statement, pointing out that a large number of Scheduled Castes residing in Calcutta Bustees have been killed [Direct Action]. At Beliaghata in Calcutta, the house of Babu Satish Chandra Bairagi, a follower of Dr Ambedkar', had been 'burnt to ashes'.

The Rajbongshis led by their leader, Premhari Burman, a member of the Bengal Legislative Assembly, lent support to the partition demand arguing that SCs were attending meetings in support of partition in large numbers and that it 'was only Mr Mandal, who was close to the League, and a few of his followers who opposed this demand'. Interestingly, a large public meeting 'was organised by the Depressed Classes League' in the University Institute Hall in Kolkata on 27 May 1947 with leaders like Babu Jagjivan Ram and Dr Rajendra Prasad in attendance. The meeting passed an emphatic resolution in support of creating a separate province by partitioning Bengal. The resolution said that since the 'Muslim League is determined to include the entire Bengal in Pakistan.... This conference resolves that a Separate Province be formed comprising the Bardwan Division, Presidency Division, Jalpaiguri, Darjeeling districts, Calcutta and other willing Units under the All India Union'. A second resolution 'rejected the "Sovereign Bengal or Free Bengal Scheme independent of the India Union". And a third condemned the activities of Mr Jogendra Nath Mandal and his baseless propaganda that the Scheduled Castes are not behind the Partition demand'. Ramananda Das, secretary of the Depressed Classes League, 'issued an appeal to all SC MLAs to cast their solid Votes in support of Bengal Partition for the best interest of the country and community'. In their detailed study titled *Caste and Partition in Bengal: The Story of Dalit Refugees, 1946–1961* (2022), Sekhar Bandyopadhyay and Anasua Basu Ray Chaudhury pointed out that on 20 June 1947, during voting in the Bengal Legislative Assembly, 'twenty-five of the thirty SC MLAs voted for the Congress-Mahasabha sponsored resolution in support of the Partition of Bengal'. Despite attempts to blanket this dimension of the creation of West Bengal by a section of scholars and ideologues, the truth is that the movement for the creation of West Bengal as a homeland for the Bengali Hindus was as much supported by the Dalit leadership and intelligentsia as it was by the upper-caste bhadralok intelligentsia. It was a demand of the Hindus of Bengal as a whole without distinction and prevarication.

What about Jogendra Nath Mandal? Mandal had to flee Pakistan within three years of its creation—beleaguered, disillusioned, battered in spirit, and politically finished. His 8,000-word resignation letter is well known and has been amply discussed. It remains a testimony to the plight of SCs in Muslim League Pakistan and justified Syama Prasad Mookerjee's prognosis on the plight of Hindus in Pakistan, his stand that the Nehru–Liaquat Pact had failed and that Pakistan had not lived up to its promises and of his call for the creation of West Bengal. Referring to the effects of Mandal's resignation letter, a letter to the editor in *Amrita Bazar Patrika* said as much:

> Mr Mandal's statement would produce three effects. In the first place, the meaning and impact of Pakistan's Islamic Policy will be clearer than ever to the world at large. Next, it will go far to vindicate Dr S.P. Mukerjee's stand that the Delhi Pact has hopelessly failed as far as Pakistan is concerned. Last of all, it will serve as a definite eye opener to Pandit Nehru who still seems to have a great faith in Mr. Liaquat Ali Khan's sincerity.

It would be relevant to cite an interview that Mandal confidentially gave to T.V. Venkatraman, the Kolkata correspondent of *The Hindu*. The details of the interview were conveyed to India. Dr Rajendra Prasad sent a copy of the interview to Sardar Patel, who had by the first week of June 1950 already received its content from the Intelligence Bureau. Patel found the document 'revealing'. The interview came within two months of the inking of the Nehru–Liaquat Pact and exposed its failure. Nehru, however, continued to ignore the reality as it was unfolding in East Bengal.

It was a transformed Mandal who lamented the fate of the Hindus of East Bengal. Mandal told Venkatraman that the 'Hindus in East Bengal to a man are emphatic that they have no place in Pakistan and are determined to leave'. He said:

> So long I have been claiming to be a representative of only the Scheduled Castes, but after what I have seen and heard, I feel I can speak for the entire Hindu community here. I have informed Delhi that it is only a question of time before the last Hindu reaches India from East Bengal. You must be prepared to receive us and rehabilitate us, and if necessary, throw out enough Muslims to make room for us. If India is not prepared to do this, we shall appeal to the world, become Buddhists, Christians, but we will not submit to a slow process of Islamisation. My idea is that there should no East Pakistan.

Mandal was beginning to repudiate his own position of a few years ago. He now warned the Nehru dispensation that 'every Muslim feels that there should be no Hindus left inside Pakistan' and that India should 'not be foolish enough to believe that after driving out the Hindus, Pakistan will live in peace with India'. Pakistan has been arming itself, buying arms from the international market and arming East Bengal. 'If in February [1950] there had been an armed intervention in East Bengal from India, it would have been all over with East Bengal, like Hyderabad, in the course of fifteen days,' Mandal observed. But his description of the plight of Hindus in East Bengal makes for an excruciating reading:

I have undertaken a long tour of East Bengal and shall remain here for a long time helping Hindus to get away from here. I have asked my followers (I represent about 25 lakhs of Scheduled Castes, mostly Namasudras) not only to resist aggression by Muslims, but to avenge thoroughly any injury done to a Hindu.... They want to drive away the Hindus from here and enjoy their property without allowing a single Muslim to enter East Bengal from India. They know that if East Pakistan is lost, Pakistan loses 12 annas in the rupee. And they know that so long as Hindus continue in East Bengal, they cannot get all that 12 annas for themselves.... I am awaiting the lead that Delhi will give to the East Bengal Hindus. I am prepared to go to Delhi and plead personally with Pandit Nehru the cause of East Bengal Hindus.... There is no propaganda by Muslims to uphold the Delhi Pact or any attempt to persuade the Hindus not to leave. The higher authorities are well-meaning, but there is a limit. If they find that one particular senior officer is taking too much interest in the Delhi Pact, they promptly transfer him.... The lower officials are bent upon frustrating the pact and any amount of orders and instructions from the top will not make them budge. They have to pander to the Muslim mentality.

Mandal told Venktraman the 'large number of instances where officialdom and Muslims alike were making life hell for the Hindus'. He said:

> Open threats are being issued to Hindus to marry their womenfolk to Muslims. Money is being extorted in the guise of giving protection to them from hooligans. If Hindus dare report to the authorities, punishment often descends upon them. Houses and crops are destroyed and women molested. Koranic prayers are to be said in every school and every Hindu is to attend standing. Indian history is being tampered with. Maharaja Nandcoomar is being mentioned as Kaffir Nandcoomar. Hindu names of schools are being changed to Muslim names. Without contributing a pie to the funds of the schools, Muslims are being given 50 per cent or more representation in the administrative bodies. In district and union board elections under joint electorates, Hindus are being terrorised not to vote so as to get as many Muslims elected as possible.

This confession and the desperate situation would eventually lead to Mandal's resignation and escape to India. In his historic resignation letter of October 1950, Mandal confessed to the debilitating effects of Direct Action on Scheduled Castes in Noakhali:

> The Calcutta carnage was followed by the 'Noakhali Riot' in October 1946. There, Hindus including Scheduled Castes were killed and hundreds were converted to Islam. Hindu women were raped and abducted. Members of my community also suffered loss of life and property. Immediately after these happenings, I visited Tipperah and Feni and saw some riot-affected areas. The terrible

sufferings of Hindus overwhelmed me with grief, but still I continued the policy of co-operation with the Muslim League.

Mandal also confessed how, even after this, his efforts enabled the Suhrawardy ministry to win the no-confidence motion brought against it in the aftermath of the Kolkata and Noakhali anti-Hindu pogroms. Mandal lamented that to his 'utter regret after partition, particularly after the death of Qaid-e-Azam, the Scheduled Castes have not received a fair deal in any matter'. Mandal listed many incidents of atrocities committed against Hindus by the Pakistani establishment, especially against the Scheduled Castes, making his letter a historic record of the agony of the minorities in Pakistan.

Among the many atrocities that he narrated against the Hindus, Mandal narrated:

the atrocities perpetrated by the police and the military on the innocent Hindus, especially the Scheduled Castes of Habibgarh in the District of Sylhet deserve description. Innocent men and women were brutally tortured, some women ravished, their houses raided and properties looted by the police and the local Muslims. Military pickets were posted in the area. The military not only oppressed these people and took away stuff forcibly from Hindu houses, but also forced Hindus to send their womenfolk at night to the camp to satisfy the carnal desires of the military. This fact also I brought to your notice. You assured me of a report on the matter, but unfortunately no report was forthcoming.

'When I am convinced that my continuance in office in the Pakistan Central Government,' Mandal told Liaquat Ali, 'is not of any help to Hindus I should not with a clear conscience, create the false impression in the minds of the Hindus of Pakistan and peoples abroad that Hindus can live there with honour and with a sense of security in respect of their life, property and religion. This is about Hindus.'

That the Dalits of Bengal played a crucial role in the formation of West Bengal is a story that has been deliberately marginalized. We have been made to forget their role and contribution in the making of the Bengali Hindu homeland because it goes against a certain imposed narrative. That the SCs have been among the most discriminated against, that they have faced religious persecution and have been driven away from Pakistan having been tortured and humiliated, is a saga that those who oppose CAA would want us to forget. The CAA and the debates it generated resurrected the memory of that persecuted and suppressed past. Those who do not speak of it do so out of sly convenience so that they can perpetuate their theories of class conflict and class dominance. That Dalits were persecuted in Pakistan is an uncomfortable truth for those who supported the theory and movement for Pakistan, especially the communists and a section of the Congress. The former, in order to erase its past record of collaboration with the Muslim League in support of its demand for Pakistan, and the latter, because it has forsaken its own past, opposed the CAA. Even after seventy-five years of partition, these parties are averse to giving justice and dignity to those Dalits and their descendants who were rendered homeless and were uprooted from the land of their ancestors and their inheritance.

5

On CAA the Congress Peddled False Narratives, Spread Misinformation, Betrayed Refugees, and Looked the Other Way

While giving his pointed replies in both houses of Parliament during the historic debate on the Citizenship Amendment Bill 2019 (9 and 12 December 2019), Union Home Minister Amit Shah asked a number of questions which the Congress and the communist parties have avoided asking in the last seven decades after India's independence. Where have the minorities of these three neighbouring countries—Pakistan, Bangladesh, and Afghanistan—gone over the years? There has been a distinct depletion of their numbers in these countries. 'Where have they gone?' Amit Shah asked the opposition benches. 'If our brothers and sisters are afflicted, face persecution and attacks in these countries, should we just look the other way? Where else will they go except come to India? Should we drive them away then?'

This was a very poignant and pertinent question. It was a fundamental one as far as the citizenship debate was concerned. That minorities were being driven out of these countries—from Pakistan, East Pakistan, and Afghanistan, especially after its Talibanization, and from post-Mujib Bangladesh, i.e. from 1975 onwards—was a fact that was well known. But it was hardly ever admitted openly in discourses the world over.

Veteran scholar of geopolitics and a former national professor Jayanta Kumar Ray, in an early study on East Pakistan and minorities (1968), said,

> Minorities in East Pakistan—Buddhists, Christians and by far the most numerous, Hindus—have been systematically discriminated against and pushed out into the neighbouring areas of India. The degree and extent of discrimination vary from time to time and place to place but it has occurred continuously.

The narrative and justification of denuding Pakistan of Hindus and other minorities began with the idea of Pakistan. Members of the Muslim intelligentsia in undivided India, while justifying the rationale of Pakistan, complained of the 'economic superiority of the Hindus' and called for a large-scale banishment of the Hindu civil servants, lawyers, businessmen, doctors, and teachers to India. In East Pakistan, too, such a migration, they argued, needed to be effectuated in order to justify the idea and meaning of Pakistan. The 'validity of this interpretation was borne out by the systematic policy of squeezing out the Hindu middle class adopted by the Pakistan government since Partition' (ibid.).

It was, therefore, Ray argued, a 'queer type of hypocrisy that Jinnah and Liaquat indulged as they bitterly criticised the Hindu intelligentsia, leaving Pakistan on the eve of

Partition, and accused them of trying, under instructions from India, to paralyze the Pakistani administrative-economic set up'. The *Dawn* which prided itself on being founded by Jinnah, wrote sometime in July 1947:

> Hindu hostility to Pakistan has manifested itself in the flight of capital and the shifting of business headquarters from Karachi and Lahore to cities in Hindustan. Behind this ill-advised and hasty act on the part of the Hindu capitalists lies the deep-seated suspicions and fear engendered by unscrupulous anti-Pakistan propagandists that the Pakistan government would either freeze or expropriate all private monies in banks and other assets. (Ispahani 2015)

Those Hindus who evacuated before Partition were prescient. They had guessed the nature of Pakistan, they smelt its intolerant Islamist fundamentalist texture. Those who stayed back would be hit by this reality within a few months.

The February 1950 pogrom which we have extensively discussed in other chapters, marked, Ray observed, 'a watershed, for it led to the complete evacuation of the Hindu intelligentsia from East Bengal'. Ray spoke of how he met a number of members of the Hindu intelligentsia who stayed back in East Bengal after Partition, 'and wanted to live there permanently, but were compelled to migrate to India after the February holocaust [1950]' which climaxed the 'unending humiliations, tortures and economic exploitation they had to face daily since the formation of Pakistan as an independent state'.

Many ways were adopted to oust the minorities of Pakistan. One most-used device to 'oust the members of the Hindu middle class was to make them homeless'. The Pakistani government launched an indiscriminate movement to requisition Hindu homes. The manner in which they executed it was horrible. Ray writes, 'An ailing old man or woman, having no other shelter, would be compelled to quit his own house at a moment's notice.' Apart from the government's arbitrariness, 'there were forcible dispossessions by Ansars and goondas enjoying official support'. When the Hindu members of the provincial Assembly complained of this, they were 'simply assured that these cases of hardship were not to be treated as a calculated assault on a particular group of people, but nothing was done to ameliorate the hardships' of the minorities. The requisition of Hindu houses both by official and non-official agencies 'proved to be a potent weapon of slowly and steadily expelling the members of the Hindu middle class'. Much the same treatment was meted out to the members of the Scheduled Castes in East Pakistan and West Pakistan.

The other method frequently adopted was the arrest and victimization of political leaders and respectable members of the minorities on the 'vague charges of anti-state activities'. Often, they were arrested for keeping photos of Gandhi and Nehru at home and 'the way arrests were executed was often strikingly inhuman and deliberately designed to sap the morale of the minorities'. Ray records, 'Old, respected leaders would be handcuffed and tied by rope to other members of [their] family while being taken to the police station through the streets'. The Pakistan government 'heaped indignities systematically on minorities by ordering widespread searches of houses. The major objective was harassment and not the discovery of incriminating materials which almost none of these searches could produce'. And harassment 'usually included molestation of women in the house'. Dr Syama Prasad Mookerjee himself testified on the floor of the Indian Parliament about these nefarious psychological techniques resorted to by Pakistan. Speaking during the historic debate on the 'Bengal Situation', Dr Mookerjee described these methods from eyewitness accounts. Sample here is testimony:

> Some of the persons who are still there [East Bengal] are the flower of our race. Many of them were Congressmen, who still cling to their faith, who are true Gandhites, perhaps better Gandhites than many in India. I have met many of them. I am sure the Prime Minister has also met at least some of them. They still consider it to be their moral right to remain in East Bengal. What happened in Barisal? I am not talking of the large-scale incidents, because if I go on with that narration, I am sure, your blood will boil. I have no desire to do that. I do not want to go to period before the 8th of April 1950 [when the Nehru-Liaquat Pact was inked]. Gentlemen like Satin Babu [Satin Sen M.L.A, East Bengal Assembly] and Durga Mohan Babu, highly respectable citizens, were asked to put down their signature to certain documents. They refused to do that. They were subsequently put under arrest. Satin Babu is a member of the East Bengal Assembly and he was arrested on a charge of murder. A man who perhaps in his whole life has never killed an ant was put under a charge of murder. He was tied with a rope with other leading Hindu gentlemen and dragged along the streets of Barisal, kept in the police station and classified as C class prisoners – dacoits, murderers, abductors of women remaining in Class I. They rightly

asked the local officials, how they were treated in this way, they expected that any Hindu would be able to live in East Bengal... The whole characteristic of the present behaviour of Pakistan is that the Hindus should be squeezed out.

These methods continued to be applied in the same manner over the next decades with the aim of persecuting and then driving out the minorities from East Pakistan into India. Pakistan's policies towards religious minorities, argues scholar-journalist Farahnaz Ispahani, is best understood by 'the Pakistan army's treatment of Bengali Hindus, who were at the time Pakistani citizens' during the genocide it perpetrated in 1971.

In Bangladesh, Hindus were at a receiving end whenever Bangladesh Nationalist Party (BNP) was in power. The regimes of Zia-Ur-Rehman between 1977 and 1981, H.M. Ershad's military dictatorship between 1983 and 1990 and the BNP regime led by Zia's widow Khaleda Zia twice from 1991 to 1996 and between 2001 and 2006 saw the maximum number of Hindus, in recent times, being compelled to flee Bangladesh. The methods, the approach, and the mindset that victimized minorities of Bangladesh and then drove them out were the same as in February 1950. Union Home Minister Amit Shah, in Parliament, had rightly referred to the persecution and displacement of Hindus from Bangladesh during the post-Mujib phase.

In 2001, the Khaleda Zia-led Bangladesh Nationalist Party (BNP) and Jamaat-e-Islami coalition came to power and unleashed a string of pogroms against minorities, especially the Hindus in Bangladesh. The series of attacks drove out a large number of Hindus who fled across the border to India. The attacks would continue throughout Zia's term. The Jamaat, led by leaders who had collaborated with Pakistan in 1971, kept egging her on to fulfil their political agenda of making Bangladesh minority-free. Among those who highlighted the plight of Hindus in Bangladesh internationally was US Congressman Frank Pallone Jr. Pallone helped put international focus on the conditions of Hindus in Bangladesh under the BNP.

In his statements in the House, Pallone described how the coalition government of the Bangladesh Nationalist Party (BNP), which had come to power in October 2001, 'has initiated a violent campaign of terrorism, murder and religious cleansing on Hindus living in Bangladesh'. Pallone spoke of how the 'latest wave of violence has been ensuing since the BNP took power in 2001 [and] Hindus have been a disappearing minority in Bangladesh at the hands of Bangladeshi forces who have employed human rights abuses, atrocities and ethno-religious cleansing tools'. Pallone highlighted how the Hindu population kept depleting over the years:

> In 1941, Hindus comprised 28% of the Bangladeshi population but by 1991, the Hindu population dwindled to a meager 8%. A large part of this decrease in the Hindu population in Bangladesh can be attributed to the 1971 genocide by the then Muslim East Pakistan Party whereby 2.5 million Hindus were murdered and 10 million Hindus fled to India as refugees.

Pallone told the house about the Khaleda Zia regime:

> Reminiscent of the Jewish holocaust, Hindu homes were marked by a yellow 'H', which in fact guided the

pillagers to their homes. Over the following 30 years, thousands of Hindu temples were destroyed, Hindus were systematically disenfranchised from holding political power, and prejudicial legislation ensured an unstable existence for Hindus. In fact, Islamic extremists have routinely dispossessed Hindus, and for that matter Christians and Buddhists, of their ancestral properties and land, burned down their houses and desecrated and razed temples, which has resulted in forcing many to flee as refugees.

In the first ten years after the independence and formation of Pakistan, the percentage of Hindus in East Pakistan fell by 6 per cent, from 28 to 22. In 1961, it further reduced to 18.5 per cent. After the liberation war and the formation of Bangladesh, this tide stemmed to a great degree. The flow of Hindus from Bangladesh to India, writes Tathagata Roy, historian and politician from West Bengal, 'came down to pre-partition levels, and it could be said that Hindus were fleeing the country in smaller numbers'.

The phase that saw Zia-ur-Rehman usurp power after Mujib's assassination, and after General Ershad, the military dictator, declared Bangladesh an Islamic country in 1989, saw renewed pogroms against Hindus, leading to a greater exodus to India. The Bharatiya Janata Party's resolution in its National Executive held at Ahmedabad between 7 and 8 October 1988 described the plight of the minorities in Bangladesh once Ershad altered the constitution to turn Bangladesh into an Islamic state. As we shall see later, BJP and its political predecessor, the Bharatiya Jana Sangh (BJS) founded by Dr Syama Prasad Mookerjee, were the only political parties which consistently spoke for the beleaguered minorities and refugees of Pakistan, and of the need to confer on them their citizenship. The Nehruvian Congress and the Congress later have always been largely silent on this front. The compulsions of their vote-bank politics have always exerted a strong veto and have shaped their stand on this civilizational issue.

The BJP's National Executive spoke of how 'Islamisation of Bangladesh has posed a serious threat to the very existence of about 20 million Hindus, Buddhists and other religious minorities'. The BJP termed Ershad's move to amend the Constitution and 'declare Islam as the religion of the State' a move that has 'transformed secular Bangladesh into a theocratic country where the life of religious minorities has been made impossible'. This was not only a negation of the Nehru–Liaquat Pact but also 'amounts to complete subversion of the 1971 revolution'. The resolution spoke of 'more than 50,000 Hindus' having 'crossed over to India during the past six months' as a 'result of the inhuman persecution by the Bangladesh administration in collusion with local Muslim fanatics'.

The BJP's document did not base itself on hearsay and instead highlighted facts and figures documented by Bangladesh-based organizations. The resolution spoke of how the migrants, a large number of students among them, were camping in the border areas of Bangladesh because they were supporters of the Awami League and faced persecution by the Ershad regime. But these were not mere political persecutions—it was another attempt to drive the minorities of Bangladesh lock, stock, and barrel into India and free up space. The students narrated 'hair-raising accounts of inhuman atrocities, of torture and extortion of money, of arrests on flimsy grounds, of destruction and desecration of temples, of organised mayhem, of abduction and rape and of terrorism in several dub-divisions of Bangladesh'. From all accounts, it was evident, the National Executive noted,

> The religious minorities (Hindus, Buddhists and Christians) have been reduced to the status of 'Zimmis' in Bangladesh. They are not permitted to worship publicly, nor can they blow conch shells or display any religious symbols outside their homes. They cannot hold any religious congregation and *kirtan*. And at the same time, study of Islamic scriptures has been made compulsory for every student.

The main objective of the new Constitution, the BJP National Executive argued, was to 'demoralise the Hindus and force them either to support Ershad or to get out. Persecution for religious and political beliefs is a flagrant violation of human rights, and the Indian people cannot remain silent spectators of this sordid drama'.

Over the years, the argument on the displaced population of minorities has found support among intellectuals within Bangladesh itself. In his widely debated book, *Political Economy of Reforming Agriculture-Land-Water Bodies in Bangladesh* (2016), noted Bangladeshi economist and public intellectual Professor Abul Barkat, has shown how, 'from 1964 to 2013, around 11.3 million Hindus left Bangladesh due to religious persecution and discrimination'. He said,

> Before the Liberation War, the daily rate of migration was 705 while it was 512 during 1971–1981 and 438 during 1981–1991, the report noted. However, it added that the number increased to 767 persons each day during 1991–2001 while around 774 persons left the country during 2001–2012.

Bangladeshi writers like Salam Azad have also written about this phenomenon. In his *Hindu Sampraday Keno Deshtyag Korchhe* (Why Hindus Are Fleeing This Country) (1999), Azad documented in great detail the atrocities on Hindus and minorities across Bangladesh between 1989 and 1997. Azad argued that the Islamization of Bangladesh's constitution paved the way for the rise of Islamists in Bangladesh, leading to the minorities becoming third-class citizens. Speaking of Bangladeshi Muslims in Delhi and West Bengal, Azad spoke of how they worked in these places, doing various jobs and returning home, having earned money. But there were no instances of Hindus who have left Bangladesh and gone to India, returning home. Muslims of Bangladesh, Azad observed, 'go to India for economic reasons, as they go to other countries', but 'Hindus do not go, they are forced to go because of discrimination and communal reasons. The poison gas of communalism pursues them till the borders of India'.

Among the reasons Azad listed, which drove minorities out of Bangladesh, were communal oppression, communal attacks, the Enemy Properties Act, occupation of lands and properties belonging to temples and other religious institutions, and the status of jobs and employment of Hindus. These reasons largely remained unchanged since the partition. Echoing many other eminent personalities from the past, Azad observes how riots always involve both sides; but in this case, one section has always been silent, been beaten up, and hounded and hunted, while the other section has only assaulted. One community has attacked the other community. The Hindu community has been beaten and assaulted by the Islamist fundamentalists. In the context of Bangladesh, therefore, these episodes can never be termed as riots. Terming them communal torture and communal attacks would be correct.

The Buddhists and Christians of Bangladesh also faced persecution during the three fundamentalist regimes of General Zia, General Ershad, and Khaleda Zia in the 1970s: 'Under President General Zia-ur Rahman, Muslim settlers were brought to colonize Hill Tracts bringing the indigenous peoples from 97% of the population in 1971 to about 50% by 1991 census. Colonisers were given free land, transport and rehabilitation funds.'

While speaking in Parliament on the history of atrocities on minorities in Bangladesh, Amit Shah argued in much the same vein when he said that minorities in Bangladesh were best protected during Bangabandhu Sheikh Mujib's period, and their condition deteriorated after that. It was bad during Pakistan's rule as well and degenerated after Mujib's assassination. Shah pointed out that since the coming to power of the Sheikh Hasina-led Awami League government, the situation had improved.

The Sheikh Hasina dispensation in Bangladesh need not pay heed to distorted versions of what Shah had said. These doctored versions were being actively dished out by a section of the communists and pseudo-secular political elements in India and worldwide. It should, instead, base its assessment and stand on Shah's statement made on the floor of the Indian Parliament. This said, the Bangladesh government ought to also accept the historical reality of discrimination and atrocities on minorities in East Pakistan, and in Bangladesh, especially during martial rule and later during the BNP rule of Khaleda Zia. The then Bangladesh High Commissioner to India, Syed Muazzem Ali had quipped in a press conference in New

Delhi 'that a person of my country would rather swim in the ocean and reach Italy instead of coming to India'. Ali, of course, knew that he was being extremely economical with the truth as well as cheeky. Intellectuals, scholars, and thinkers from his own country had well documented the persecution of minorities in Bangladesh and the economic reasons that drove Bangladeshis to India. On the Indian side, such officers and constitutional heads with a stellar record of services such as General S.K. Sinha, former Governor of Assam and Bihar, T.V. Rajeshwar, former director of the Intelligence Bureau and later Governor of the Indian state of West Bengal and Uttar Pradesh, and General Ajai Singh, former Governor of Assam, to name a few, have all well documented the effects of illegal infiltration from Bangladesh—social, political and economic—on the border states of India. For the Bangladeshi infiltrator, it was easier to swim across a border pond into West Bengal and Assam rather than swim across oceans to reach Italy!

On the definition of secularism, Amit Shah asked the Opposition, how is it that 'just because this Bill does not speak of Muslims, you dub it as anti-secular, but you do not see that it includes all minorities in the countries mentioned. Why don't you see that it speaks of Christians, Sikhs, Jains, Parsis, Buddhists as well?' Shah also pointed out how this Bill was meant to confer citizenship and not take it away. He went on to state a number of times on the floor of Parliament that Muslims who are citizens of India had nothing to be apprehensive of and should not fall for false propaganda spread by a section of the opposition which said that their citizenship would be snatched away by this Act.

The CAA, both Shah and Modi time and again pointed out, does not take citizenship away, but was meant to 'give citizenship to religiously persecuted refugees, it is not to take away citizenship of any Indian'. At the height of the debate, a section of the opposition parties tried to interpret it otherwise, imparting it a majority-versus-minority angle. For instance, when the ruling Trinamool Congress in West Bengal pushed through an anti-CAA resolution in the state Assembly, the Communist Party of India Marxist (CPIM) legislative party leader Sujan Chakraborty openly said that the Act was 'anti-Muslim' while West Bengal Chief Minister Mamata Banerjee, deftly avoided terming it 'anti-Muslim', said that it was a 'shame on humanity'.

However, Banerjee was also the only elected chief minister of a state to strangely call for a United Nations referendum on the issue. Addressing an anti-CAA rally in Kolkata, Banerjee in a fit of excitement told the gathering that, 'Just because BJP has got the majority doesn't mean they can do whatever they want. If the BJP has guts, it should go for a United Nations monitored referendum on the issue of the Citizenship Amendment Act and the NRC', and if it loses the mass vote, Banerjee told her belligerent audience, it must step down. Clearly, she had overstepped her Constitutional brief by calling for a UN referendum on a law that was debated and enacted by the Indian Parliament and given assent to by the President of the Indian Republic. As early as the first week of March 2020, when the world had been alerted to the threat of Covid and Prime Minister Modi had already launched massive preparations to tackle it, Mamata Banerjee preposterously claimed that the Covid alert was a ruse by the Modi government to divert attention from the anti-CAA clashes in Delhi. Both Modi and Shah, on the other hand, repeatedly asserted in various forums, programmes, and rallies that the CAA was not meant to take away but to confer citizenship.

In January 2020, Mamata Banerjee's party, the Trinamool Congress, under her direction, passed an anti-CAA resolution in the West Bengal Assembly. Though the resolution was more a piece of propaganda and showmanship since it did not stand legal and constitutional ground against a law passed by the Indian Parliament, it was nevertheless ironical that the floor of the West Bengal Assembly, which had voted in favour of creating a Hindu homeland seventy-five years ago in 1947, would witness the passing of a resolution that meant to block Bengali Hindus from coming away and finding shelter in West Bengal in case of religious persecution across the border. The communist government of Kerala and the Congress governments of Punjab and Rajasthan also passed similar resolutions.

One thing became evident and that was that the anti-CAA protestors tied themselves up in knots, and had, by colluding with groups that were inimical to India's national interest, ensured that their protests were taken control of by such elements. Union Home Minister Amit Shah, disclosed in his reply to the Lok Sabha, that three financiers of the anti-CAA protests had been rounded up and that the conspiracy to defame India or to destabilize her internally was not just a home-grown effort but had international dimensions.

By encouraging violent opposition to the granting of citizenship to a few persecuted people from certain religious denominations from India's neighbourhood, the anti-CAA cackle adopted a rabid communal stance and alienated the vast majority. The vast majority of Indians were surprised at the needless ferocity of these protests. Not that the ferocity served any purpose, and eventually most of the protests were left high and dry. But what was worrying was how a certain section among the political, intellectual, and academic classes wilfully fanned the fires of violent protest. Their attitude and approach boded ill for the future of Indian parliamentary democracy.

Harsh Mander, a former National Advisory Council (NAC) member, known as a close confidante and policy advisor to former Congress president Sonia Gandhi, repeatedly indulged in speeches asking for settling the CAA issue and the Article 370 abrogation issue on the streets. Mander said this issue could not be settled or decided by the Supreme Court of India or the Parliament and demanded from the protestors that they settle the matter on the streets. He imparted a clever twist to his basic demand for rejecting India's constitutional institutions by saying that ultimately the issue would be settled in 'our hearts'.

How come, if that was to be the case, Mr Mander's heart did not hear the cry of the poor refugees from Pakistan, how come his heart did not respond to the spine-chilling wails of the Hindu minorities in Pakistan, East Pakistan, and Bangladesh? How come, in his three decades of public activism, Mr Mander has not once spoken of the oppressed and persecuted minorities of Pakistan and of the Bengali Hindus who have been driven away from their ancestral lands? How come he and his political masters did not frame a policy through the NAAC that could provide relief to the beleaguered minorities from India's neighbourhood? What Mr Harsh Mander had actually meant through his pseudo-Gandhian speech in Jamia was to express support for violence and mobocracy to take over the spirit of democratic protest, dialogue, and debate.

Earlier, Congress president Sonia Gandhi and Rahul Gandhi, Mander's political mentors and benefactors, both members of Parliament, had called for people to hit the streets, to come out and protest against CAA. This violently revanchist call was given on 14 December, and as Union Home Minister Amit Shah pointed out, the Shaheen Bagh protests began on 16 December 2019.

In its 2019 Vision Document released during the election campaign, the BJP had clearly stated its intent of bringing about the Citizenship Amendment Bill. Since its early years, the BJS, and later the BJP, have always advocated the need for providing citizenship to these beleaguered minorities of Pakistan, to protect them, and to fulfil the promise India made to them at the time of partition.

Jana Sangh's first inaugural all-India session on 21 October 1951 under the presidency of Dr Syama Prasad Mookerjee spoke of giving 'top priority' to the 'problem of rehabilitation of displaced persons'. For the Jana Sangh, the 'rehabilitation of those who have suffered from partition and come over to *Bharat* is legally as well as morally the responsibility of *Bharat* which must not be side-tracked'. The BJS spoke of the 'sacred duty of Bharat to secure to the minorities of Pakistan to whom the Pakistan Government had failed to accord reasonable security of life and property' and 'honourable existence', 'a civilised living with equality and honour'. This was a demand that the Jana Sangh stuck to for decades.

In its 2014 Vision Document, the BJP stated, 'India shall remain a natural home for persecuted Hindus and they shall be welcome to seek refuge here (40).' In its 2019 Vision Document, the BJP clearly stated,

> We are committed to the enactment of the Citizenship
> Amendment Bill for the protection of individuals of
> religious minority communities from neighbouring
> countries escaping persecution. We will make all efforts
> to clarify the issues to the sections of population from the
> North-eastern states who have expressed apprehension
> regarding the legislation. We reiterate our commitment
> to protect the linguistic, cultural and social identity of
> the people of the Northeast. Hindus, Jains, Buddhists,
> Sikhs and Christians escaping from India's neighbouring
> countries will be given citizenship in India. (12)

It was with this Vision Document that the BJP went into
elections in 2019 and won a historic majority. By pushing
through the CAA in December 2019 and getting Parliament
to debate and pass it, the BJP had simply kept its promise
made over decades. It had adhered to each section of the
promise it had made in its Vision Document of 2019.

Most BJP watchers, BJP critics, and baiters had
overlooked this aspect. They had not anticipated that
the BJP would resolutely go ahead with fulfilling one
of its principal promises the moment it saw a window
of opportunity. The hue and cry from a section among
these once the CAA was passed was, therefore, surprising
and betrayed a dual standard when it came to assessing
the BJP. The cause of the refugees and the need to grant
them citizenship was continuously referred to in party
programmes, party resolutions and meetings, and by the
party's leaders in the Parliament. Deendayal Upadhyaya
himself wrote extensively and prolifically on the issue,
while leaders like Atal Bihari Vajpayee kept the issue alive,
for decades, within the legislature. Most had expected

that the BJP would routinely include such a promise in its manifesto but never attempt to fulfil it. They were used to the old politics of making major promises but never fulfilling them, popularized by the Congress culture. They were proved wrong in the case of the BJP.

There is enough evidence to show the plight of the minorities in Pakistan and the circumstances and policies that evicted them from their lands. The BJP's Vision Document, therefore, was not referring to an issue that did not exist. It was an issue that burnt but one which most vote-bank-obsessed political parties would not want to see or acknowledge.

Speaking of the conditions of minorities in Pakistan in recent years, Farahnaz Ispahani, argues,

> To say that Pakistan's religious minorities are under attack is a self-evident truth. Pakistani laws, especially ones that deal with blasphemy, deny or interfere with the practice of minority faiths. Religious minorities are targets of legal as well as social discrimination. Most significantly, in recent years, Pakistan has witnessed some of the worst organized violence against religious minorities since the 1947 Partition.

She points out, 'Non-Muslim minorities such as Christians, Hindus, and Sikhs have been victims of suicide bomb attacks on their neighbourhoods, and their community members have been converted to Islam against their will.' When a semblance of democracy came to Pakistan in 2013 with the election of Nawaz Sharif's PML (N), it did not improve the situation for minorities. 'For them, the ever-present threats of violence, prosecution for blasphemy and persecution under discriminatory laws remained, just as they had, in varying degrees of consequence, since independence,' Ispahani writes. Pakistan's 'national discourse, aided by its school curriculum, generates religious prejudice against minorities'. Prejudice against minorities is ingrained in the Pakistani system which makes sure that it is renewed with every generation. Amalendu Misra, professor of international politics at the University of Lancaster and an author, writes in *Life in Brackets: Minority Christians and Hegemonic Violence in Pakistan* (2015) that in the 'last decade, children in most state-run educational establishments were expected to recite every day "*Pakistan ka matlab kya? La illaha illala!* (What is the meaning of Pakistan? There is no god but Allah!)"' Speaking of Pakistan's Christian minorities, Misra points out that, on a regular basis, they have been subjected to 'arson attacks, lynching, mob violence, demonisation through Friday religious prayers, rape of Christian women, kidnapping of Christian girls and forcing their conversion to Islam, land grabbing, destruction of Christian religious buildings, public humiliation, kidnapping, extra-judicial killing, false accusations, eviction and target killings'.

On CAA, Pakistan indulged in a vicious anti-India campaign globally. Experts spoke of Pakistan's 'insidious attempt to incite the Muslims of India' when the CAA debate raged across the country. Trying to hide its abysmal and abominable record of protecting its minorities, the Pakistan establishment led by the ISI peddled the narrative that the CAA was a:

Weapon—disguised in legal language—to permanently disenfranchise India's Muslims; that Indian Muslims are under assault; they know it is a do or die situation for them; they are well aware that silence over the matter of citizenship is nothing short of enabling the government to ghettoise them and this would lead to dangerous sectarian violence.

The Pak foreign office termed the CAA as 'driven by a toxic mix of an extremist "Hindutva" ideology and hegemonic ambitions in the region'. Was the Pak establishment echoing the views of the Indian Opposition led by the Congress or was it the other way around was a point that needed to be examined.

One of the foremost Pakistan experts in India, Tilak Devasher, pointed out that the Pakistan media and leaders 'deliberately obfuscated' the fact that the 'CAA does not take away citizenship of any Indian irrespective of her or his faith'. The Indian leadership has reiterated that all that the CAA does 'is to accelerate the process of giving citizenship to those religious minorities from selected countries who are persecuted'. Anyone, 'regardless of faith', Devasher argued, 'can continue to seek Indian citizenship through the regular procedure as before'. Pakistan was intruding into India's internal affairs, just so that it could cover up its atrocious records on the rights of minorities.

Pakistan's own record on the treatment of minorities is reminiscent of Nazi Germany's treatment of Jews. Basing himself on data from the Human Rights Commission of Pakistan, Devasher says that 'over 1000 girls belonging to religious minorities are forcibly converted to Islam every year'. Hindu temples, Christian churches and Ahmadi mosques have been regularly attacked and bombed, while members of their community have 'been killed, their

women raped and forcibly converted to Islam'. Hindu
traders and moneylenders are regularly kidnapped for
ransom, while blasphemy laws are used mainly against
minorities. In the minority right index, 'Pakistan ranks as
the ninth worst country.' The abduction of minor girls from
minority communities, their forcible conversion to Islam,
and their forcible marriage to their abductors comprise
the norm and routine in Pakistan. Fifteen-year-old Hindu
girl Mehak Kumari of Abbottabad, 13-year-old Raveena,
15-year-old Reema, Christians Huma Masih and Sadaf,
both 13 years old, and the 16-year-old Sikh Jagjit Kaur, are
only a few names that have come to the surface of victims
of these acts of abduction and forcible conversion to Islam.
Devasher writes,

> [According] to a July 2005 report released by the Aurat
> Foundation, about 1,000 forced conversions took place
> in Pakistan annually. Majority of these were in Sindh,
> where the overwhelming majority forcibly converted were
> Hindus. Another report of the University of Birmingham
> in 2018 stated that evidence provided by NGOs, journalists
> and academics showed that 'in most cases, the victim is
> abducted and is then subjected to sustained emotional and
> physical abuse, often involving threats of violence towards
> their loved ones'. According to the university, no less than
> 20 Hindu girls are kidnapped and proselytised every month
> in Pakistan.

Samson Salamat, member of the Pakistan-based National
Commission for Justice and Peace, while speaking at the
United Nations Commission for Human Rights working
group on minorities in March 2004 mentioned that
'continued incidents of violence against religious minority

groups, attacks and destruction of their places of worship, killing and rape of the members of minority communities' was a matter of grave concern. Salamat told the working group that the 'alarming situation' of the minorities in Pakistan was 'partly due to the apathy on the part of the successive governments and partly because in Pakistan a number of laws and policies exist which give preferential treatment to the majority religious group. The minority religious communities face infringement of civil and political rights as well as economic, social, and cultural rights due to this religious discrimination.'

Amalendu Misra makes some very interesting observations on violence against minorities, especially Christians, in this case. Misra writes that in recent decades, 'direct and indirect egregious majoritarian violence against Christians' in Pakistan has 'become persistent and widespread'. The violence was countrywide, rural and urban, and 'involves both *ad hoc i.e.*, apparently spontaneous acts of attack, as well as *organised* anti-Christian purges in which government authorities, local and national, collude either directly or by omission'. Misra argues that 'both formal and informal discrimination against minorities has gone hand in hand; one has encouraged and deepened the other'.

Zulfikar Ali Bhutto and his Pakistan's Peoples Party, while nationalising schools and colleges, writes Misra, 'introduced laws and policies that encouraged discrimination against the country's minorities'. Although, as we have seen, tolerance towards minorities saw a sustained erosion since the 1950s. Misra argues that 'Bhutto's intervention was the first sustained official attempt to ostracise all non-Muslim minorities from the national mainstream.' General Zia ul-Haq's rule between

1977 and 1988, saw a further depletion of minorities and their rights in Pakistan. Zia spoke of Pakistan as an 'ideological state' held together and defined by Islam. 'Take Islam out of Pakistan,' Zia once quipped, 'and make it a secular state; it would collapse.'

The modus operandi of the Pakistan state today vis-à-vis its minorities is the same as when it was founded. Police continue to 'refuse to register FIR' and 'falsify information, thereby denying families the chance to take their case any further'. While the judiciary,

> both lower and higher courts, tend to accept the claims about supposed free will. There is often no investigation into the circumstances under which the conversion took place and the age of the girl is ignored. The girl involved is often left in the custody of her kidnapper throughout the trial process where she is subjected to further threats to force her into denying her abduction and rape and accepting that the conversion was voluntary.

The Asian Human Rights Commission has recorded how a number of local mosques encourage the conversion of minorities through rewards. They pass these illegal criminal acts as 'official policy'. The local imams and other Islamist outfits have likened the act of converting the minorities to Islam as the 'equivalent of "Haj-e-Akbari", or the greatest religious duty of Muslims that will bring reward in *"akhirat"* (hereafter)'.

If one were to look at the key challenges that the minorities face in Pakistan today, they are the same as those faced by the minorities of the newly formed Pakistan state seven decades ago. Devasher lists these:

The key issues facing the minorities in Pakistan are that compared to their population, they are disproportionately targeted with false accusations under the blasphemy laws; their homes and places of worship are frequently attacked by mobs and nobody is brought to justice; their women and especially underage girls are forcibly converted and married off to Muslim men. During the coronavirus pandemic, cases have surfaced when minorities were deprived of food and forced to convert to Islam to receive sustenance.

A Sindh-based minority rights activist Sufi Munawar Laghari, describing the conditions of the minorities in Pakistan says, 'Hindus do not have much choice in the political scheme of Pakistan. They have to convert and leave ancestral lands to save lives. In many cases, the less abled elderly and infants are immolated inside homes and temples when Muslim brigades set fire to their neighbourhoods.'

The Hindus of Pakistan bore the brunt of affront and insult even during the deadly COVID pandemic when many Islamic scholars in Sindh blamed the spread of the virus on the 'immoral and filthy lifestyle' of the Hindus. During Covid, Hindus in Pakistan were denied ration, water, and shelter. Often these were used as a pretext to coerce Hindus into converting to Islam. In Sukkur, for instance, 'Muslim goons beat and severely injured more than a dozen Hindu women and children for drinking water from a "Muslim" pump.' The Pak government, by design, denied the basics to the Hindus during the pandemic, while 'pious Muslims refused to offer food during the lockdown.' When Shias and some Shia organisations attempted to provide relief to Hindus, they faced a backlash and were accused of sacrilege by extremist organisations which were given a free run.

The inhuman conditions under which Hindus survive in Pakistan today are painfully described by Dr Lakhu Lohana of the World Sindhi Congress. He says:

> Madrassahs have become the source to formalize sex slavery in the name of serving religion. It is common for such Madrassahs to invite media and local crowds to cheer conversion ceremonies. Crowds celebrate the solemnisation rites with chants of Allah O Akbar to register Islam's victory over Hindu religion and community. These converted minors often find themselves tethered to a man three times their age and already married with two or three wives. Hindu girls who resist rape and forced conversion are at high risk of murders. These children are permanently severed from their families and roots. Those few who manage to escape to their parents cannot revert to Hinduism as leaving Islam is judicial execution under Pakistani law, often by stoning to death. Any attempt by Hindu parents to reclaim their girls is deemed blasphemous, which is also a capital punishment in Pakistan. Those accused of blasphemy walk with a death warrant and often face mob lynching and target killing before they make it to the court of law.

For Lohana, 'persecution and expulsion of Hindus from Sindh is part of Pakistan's grand designs'. He says,

> [It is] as appalling as it sounds; all State institutions are in it together and there is no punishment for the perpetrators and no justice for the victims. It is not too hard to uncover the paradox in their moral standards as same Pakistani rulers will leave no stone unturned defending land and religious rights of Kashmiri and Palestinian Muslims.

While the 198-feet-tall Bochasanwasi Akshar Purushottam Swaminarayan Sanstha (BAPS) Hindu temple, the first of its kind in the Middle East, saw a grand inauguration in February 2024 at Abu Dhabi by Prime Minister Narendra Modi, in Pakistan, attempts to construct the first Hindu temple in Islamabad, perhaps the first in Pakistan since 1947, 'had to be halted when several clerics and even politicians objected to its construction with Muslim taxes in an "Islamic Republic". Subsequently, zealots demolished the unfinished wall of the temple'. In contrast, the United Arab Emirates (UAE) government announced that it would donate land for the temple with the ruler of Abu Dhabi, Sheikh Mohammed bin Zayed Al Nahyan, graciously gifting the land in 2018. While in Pakistan, 'a religious group forcibly occupied the land of Gurdwara Shahidi Asthan Bhai Taru Singh, Lahore. The gurdwara is the site of the martyrdom of Bhai Taru Singh in 1745'. The land-grabbers claimed the 'place for Masjid Shahid Ganj and tried to convert it into a mosque'.

The *Dawn*, which had once sung Jinnah and Liaquat Ali's tune and had castigated the Hindus in July 1947 for leaving Karachi and Lahore and relocating to cities in India, now lamented the plight of the minorities in Pakistan: 'Pakistan's minorities often live under a cloud of fear and insecurity.... Instead of receiving protection, vulnerable groups are ignored or thrown under the bus, over and over again, as they navigate layers of systemic discrimination and deeply rooted cultural biases...'. It is a lament that has come too late; Pakistan's depleting minorities have relentlessly faced the steamroller and crusher for seven decades. The CAA offered them an opportunity for a dignified existence in India, their civilizational home. It was appalling, therefore, to see the vehemence with which the Congress and the communist parties and their intellectual drum-beaters were opposing the passage of the CAA.

The relevance of the CAA became evident within a few months of it being passed by the Indian Parliament. On 25 March 2020, an attack on the Gurdwara Har Rai Sahib in Kabul which killed twenty-five Sikhs shook the minorities of Afghanistan. They appealed to the Indian government to evacuate them. According to historians, there were at least 2,00,000 Hindus and Sikhs in Afghanistan till the 1970s. In 1988, during the Baisakhi festivities, a gunman with an AK-47 mowed down thirteen Sikhs in a gurdwara in Jalalabad; in 1989, the Jalalabad-based Gurdwara Guru Teg Bahadur Singh was hit by a rocket fired by the Mujahideen killing seventeen Sikhs. It was after Kabul fell to the Mujahideen and the execution of President Najibullah that the Sikhs and Hindus of Afghanistan were forced to leave in large numbers.

> Under the Mujahideen, there were widespread kidnappings, extortion, property grabbing incidents, religious persecution, targeting Sikhs and Hindus which became the trigger point for exodus. After the Taliban took over Afghanistan, those who remained continued to face persecution.

A suicide bomb attack in Jalalabad in July 2018 killed nineteen Sikhs and Hindus. But the 25 March 2020 attack was the breaking point. Gurdwaras are targeted in Afghanistan because most Sikhs live in them, having no separate houses for themselves.

In August 2021, in a bold and swift move, Prime Minister Narendra Modi, responding to the appeals of the Sikhs and Hindus of Afghanistan, ordered their evacuation. In the Cabinet Committee on Security (CCS) meeting that Modi chaired, he asserted,

> India must not only protect our citizens, but we must also provide refuge to those Sikh and Hindu minorities who want to come to India, and we must also provide all possible help to our Afghan brothers and sisters who are looking towards India for assistance.

The Congress governments of the past had repeatedly ignored the plight of the Sikhs and Hindus of Afghanistan and Pakistan. Through a web of false propaganda and misinformation, they would want us to forget that past.

6

Communist Perfidy on CAA

The communist parties of India have a history of being the proponents and supporters of separatism. Historically, they have sided with forces which represent, articulate, or symbolize separatist tendencies and ideologies. This essential standpoint has often led them to voice support for separatists in Kashmir and for the Islamist radicals in Tamil Nadu, Kerala, and West Bengal. They are also at the forefront of organizing international propaganda against India whenever they find an opportunity to do so.

The arrest of Taha Faizal and Alan Suhaib, both active Communist Party of India (Marxist) [CPI(M)] members, in November 2019 from Pantheerankavu near Kozhikode, for distributing Maoist pamphlets clearly proved that there was a live link between Islamists and Maoists. That a section among the CPI(M) cadres is active in keeping that link alive came to light with the arrest of Faizal and Suhaib. In the anti-CAA protests across the country, the CPI(M) played a major role. It provided ballast to elements who, having infiltrated and engineered these protests, aimed at generating unrest and creating zones of conflict across the country.

Splinter parties like the Communist Party of India (Marxist–Leninist) [CPI(ML)] and its violence-prone student outfit the All India Students' Association (AISA), which used to celebrate each time Indian security force personnel were attacked, killed, or maimed in terror attacks, all joined hands to oppose CAA. They were hell-bent on trying to prevent the granting of citizenship to the large number of Dalit refugees who were forced to flee religious persecution in Pakistan. By opposing CAA, not only was CPI(M) and its other communist partners taking a stand which was anti-parliament and unconstitutional, but it was also wilfully partnering with India-wrecking forces. A diminishing electoral footprint is not its concern; it is obsessed rather with ensuring that these regressive forces gain strength. That said, let us have a look at the hypocrisy of the left political conglomerate about the CAA.

Let us start from the past. At the time of partition, it is interesting to note, as Prafulla Chakrabarti states in his seminal work *Marginal Men: The Refugees and the Left Political Syndrome in West Bengal* (1999) that the 'Communist Party refused to accept the existence of the luckless victims of communal hatred'. In their dialectical wisdom, the leaders of the CPI decided that after partition there would be 'one Party for both Dominions'. The comrades in Pakistan were therefore directed not to migrate to India. Krishna Binode Roy and Mansur Habibullah from West Bengal were sent to organize the party in East Bengal while Sajjad Zaheer was sent to West Pakistan. 'These three communists were arrested within a month of their arrival in Pakistan.' Other 'important Communists of East Pakistan' writes Chakrabarti, 'were sent to jail' and those other 'well-known party members who came over to West Bengal disregarding the party mandate were promptly expelled'. In his *Eclipse of East Pakistan*, Jyoti Sengupta writes that 'The Pakistan Party [Pakistan Communist Party] has been subject to intense governmental repression since the founding of Pakistan...' He says,

> The Communist Party was virtually under ban since the birth of Pakistan. Hundreds of its workers were in detention or were serving prison terms. Many went underground as there were warrants of arrest pending against them. The Party, no doubt, took part in the elections of [1954] but it had no funds nor could it do any electioneering as its meetings were banned.

Yet, the communists of today have a habit of singing paeans to Pakistan!

In the decade before partition, the communist party became active in the region which later formed Pakistan. In East Bengal, the party comprised mostly of middle-class Hindus, and over the years leading to partition, these leaders had managed to build up 'small and disparate Communist pockets among the peasantry and tribals in different parts of East Bengal'. When the communist-led Tebhaga movement—a peasant uprising—was seen picking up steam in East Pakistan, the government of East Pakistan 'lost no time in eliminating those small and disparate pockets of Communist influence'. Members of the Scheduled Tribe (ST) communities such as Garos, Hajongs, and Dalus from Susang in Netrakona of East Bengal, active in the Tebhaga movement, were expelled and pushed to India's northeast in Meghalaya. The 'peasantry of Dinajpur and Rajshahi districts', noted Chakrabarti, 'who joined the Tebhaga movement under Communist leadership were subjected to police repression and terrorised into submission'. Yet, the communist dictate was that the 'comrades must not move out of East Pakistan' (1999).

The communists were at the forefront of the demand for Pakistan. They were one of the staunchest allies of the Muslim League in its countrywide agitation for a Muslim homeland. In the crucial decade of the 1940s, the communists worked closely with the Muslim League. The CPI 'raised its voice against the partition of Bengal, although it supported the proposal of Pakistan with Bengal as a part of the new state,' writes Nitish Sengupta, scholar-administrator, in his *Bengal Divided: the Unmaking of a Nation – 1905–1971*. Comrade Jyoti Basu got elected to the Bengal Legislative Assembly in 1946 from the Saidpur Railwaymen Constituency with the help of the Muslim League. H.S. Suhrawardy, the then Muslim League premier of Bengal, who had directed the Calcutta killings on Direct Action Day, played a crucial role in getting Basu elected. The Muslim League 'lending whole-hearted support to the Communist, had preferred not to put up any candidate'. The League hoodlums 'assaulted and severely injured Basu's opponent from the Krishak Praja Party, Humayun Kabir, a leading Bengali intellectual and educationist, who would go on to become India's education minister, at Bhairab Bazar station in East Bengal before abducting him'. Kabir was kept captive for a fortnight and released only after Basu had won by a slender margin. The communist–League camaraderie was indeed deep-seated.

Between 1943 and 1946, the communists threw their strength behind the Muslim League in its propaganda for Pakistan. In a resolution in September 1942 at the Plenum of its Central Committee, the CPI argued,

> Every section of the Indian people which has a contiguous territory as its homeland, common historical tradition, common language, culture, psychological make-up, and common economic life would be recognised as a distinct nationality with the right to exist as an autonomous state within the free Indian Union or federation and will have the right to secede from it if may so desire ... free India of tomorrow would be a federation or union of autonomous states of the various nationalities such as the Pathans, Western Punjabis (dominantly Muslims), Sikhs, Sindhis, Hindustanis, Rajasthanis, Gujeratis, Bengalis, Assamees, Beharis, Oriyas, Andhras, Tamils, Karnatikas, Maharashtrians, Keralas, etc.

In its election manifesto of 1946, the party called for power to be transferred to seventeen different 'sovereign national constituent assemblies' rather than to India and Pakistan. The seventeen new nations were described as the party in 1942. The communist leaders instructed its cadres to fan out across the country in support of the Muslim League's demand for Pakistan. 'To the Hindu masses,' they argued, 'we must explain that what is just in this Pakistani demand, namely the right of the Muslim nationalities to autonomous state existence', including the right to separation. The communist party organs were instructed to portray the Muslim League and Jinnah as progressive.

The communist support to Pakistan can be traced back to as early as 1941 when they began organizing public meetings in support of the Pakistani idea. In their well-documented work, *The Sickle and the Crescent: Communists, Muslim League and India's Partition* (2011), Sunanda Sanyal and Soumya Basu have traced this communist–Muslim League partnership over the demand for Pakistan.

In May 1941, for instance, the Students Federation and Muslim Students League organized a meeting in Kolkata's Shraddhanand Park in support of the Pakistan demand. Nikhil Maitra of the Student's Federation, in his presidential address, pleaded with the gathering that 'we should not condemn our Muslim friends for their proposal for Pakistan. If we consider calmly and soberly, we shall understand that every nation has got its own right to culture his own religion, education etc'. Pakistan Day celebrations were observed across Bengal, especially East Bengal in 1944, jointly by the League's outfits and the CPI's frontal organizations. These meetings ended with the chants of 'Pakistan Zindabad'. A letter to the editor of the communist mouthpiece *People's War* dated 25 March 1944, written by one Phani Guha, of the Dhaka district committee of the CPI, for instance, argued that the 'demand for Pakistan and India's freedom movement are not contradictory but have roots in the same freedom urge of the people of India, that was expressed when Pakistan Day was observed in Dacca City on March 23'. Ten thousand people participated in Pakistan Day celebrations in Chittagong in March 1944, organized by the Muslim League. Among the speakers were:

> Comrade Jashoda Chakravarty, secretary of the Communist Party in Chittagong, Comrade Kalpana Dutt, president of Nari Samiti, who was once among the leading lights of the Chittagong revolt under the leadership of 'Masterda' Surya Sen and Comrade Madhu Singh, secretary of the All-India Students Federation. The meeting ended with cries of 'Pakistan Zindabad' and 'Muslim League Zindabad'.

One Annada Shankar Bhattacharya, secretary of the Bengal Provincial Students' Federation, wrote to his all-India secretary describing the 'kind of support the local League was providing to the meetings of the Communists'. Bhattacharya wrote that the League was 'actively cooperating with us' and 'is always pressing to call joint meetings'. The communists actively collaborated with the Muslim League in organizing Jinnah Day on Jinnah's birthday in 1945 across the country including in Bengal. In Lahore, for instance, at a public programme on Jinnah Day, Balraj Mehta, 'a prominent member of Punjab's Students Federation' addressing a gathering at the Islamia College Hall sang paeans to Jinnah. Mr Jinnah, Mehta declared, 'is anti-imperialist and not anti-Congress. His life has been a relentless struggle for achievements of three objectives – Freedom of India, Hindu-Muslim understanding and the birthright of the Muslims, i.e. Pakistan.'

Despite all their grovelling support for him and his vain dream of Pakistan, Jinnah was contemptuous of communists. He told the Muslim League session in Lahore, to bursts of claps and roar of laughter,

> I find that the cleverest party that is carrying on propaganda are the Communists. They have got so many flags, and I think they consider that there is safety in numbers. They have got the Red flag; they have got the Russian flag, they have got the Soviet flag, they have got the Congress flag. And now they have been good enough to introduce our flag also…. Well, when a man has too many flags, I get suspicious.

Of the communist support for Pakistan, Dr Rammanohar Lohia has perhaps best described it.

> Communist support to partition did not produce Pakistan. At its worst it acted like an incubator. Nobody remembers

it now except as a stale propagandist argument against communism. I am somewhat intrigued by this aspect of communist treachery, that it leaves no lasting bad taste in the mouth of the people. Other traitors are not so fortunate. (2000)

In their detailed work *Religion and Politics in Bangladesh and West Bengal: A Study of Communal Relation* (1993), Sukumar Biswas and Hiroshi Sato give a graphic description of what happened to comrades and their tribal cadres whom they led in East Pakistan in 1950:

> Village after village was indiscriminately burnt down, peasants were beaten and tortured mercilessly. They created a reign of terror by free looting, and raping of the Santal women went at will. 24 Santal peasants succumbed to death due to police torture inside Nachole [Rajshahi division] police station. Innumerable peasants were killed in Nawabganj and Rajshahi Jails. One of the notable leaders of the movement Ila Mitra [leader of the CPI, leading the Santals in the Tebhaga movement] was brutally tortured in several ways including rape. The pervasive and multi-directional torturing compelled several Santal peasants to emigrate to West Bengal.

Biswas and Sato are cited by A.J. Kamra, in his deeply disturbing book, *The Prolonged Partition and Its Pogroms: Testimonies on Violence against Hindus in East Bengal 1946–64* (2000), a comprehensively documented volume on how the minorities were driven away from Pakistan over the years through a systematic cycle of attack and torture by the Muslim-League-controlled Pakistani establishment. Comrade Ila Mitra was imprisoned for life in East Pakistan, severely tortured, and released on parole in 1954, only when her health had completely collapsed. She came to Kolkata for treatment and never went back; she could not as communists had no place in Pakistan and could only survive in India. Mitra went on to become a Member of the West Bengal Legislative Assembly.

Even when the influx from East Pakistan had 'reached formidable proportions', clearly indicating that minority Hindus had no place in Pakistan, 'the Communist Party,' argues Chakrabarti, 'hardly gave any thought to this overwhelming mass of suffering humanity. There was no attempt at a serious Marxist analysis of this new phenomenon and a clear definition of the attitude of the Party towards the refugees.'

The disconcerting saga of Ila Mitra and her comrades is perhaps no more narrated in communist party classes since their story is difficult to explain to cadres who are fed on daily doses of how India is turning into a 'Hindu fascist republic'. Comrade D. Raja, Comrade Binoy Viswam, and Comrade Sitaram Yechury—leading lights of the communist movement in India—may not have heard of Ila Mitra. Even if they have, they prefer to nudge the memory of her ordeal into shelves of oblivion.

At a time when they were siding with Islamist radicals, at a time when they were parroting Pakistan's version of CAA, at a time when they were exerting their energies to push the PFI agenda, at a crucial time when they were marching in solidarity with stone pelters of Jamia and the Bangladeshi rioters of Seelampur in Delhi, how could they speak of Comrade Ila Mitra, her life, her struggles, her torture in Pakistan, her imprisonment, and dishonour? She stands as an antithesis to the communists' cacophony against CAA and therefore she must be forgotten, her memory silenced.

While speaking of the ordeals of the socialist and left leaders in Pakistan, it would be relevant, for instance, to recall the experiences of Professor Samar Guha, one of the most well-known acolytes of Netaji Subhas Chandra Bose and a legendary leader who did much to preserve Netaji's memory and contribution. He was once a leading light of the Forward Bloc in East Pakistan, and later, a close associate of Jayaprakash Narayan. Guha also became a Member of the Lok Sabha in 1977. He had remained in East Pakistan after partition, was imprisoned in Dhaka, and finally was forced to come away to India in 1951. Towards his last phase, Guha gravitated towards the Janata Dal (Secular) [JD(S)].

In his book *Non-Muslims Behind the Curtain in Pakistan*, Guha writes,

A year of Pakistan rolled over. Soon a complete reversal of government policy towards the Hindus became glaringly manifest. East Bengal police suddenly became very active with repressive measures against the non-Muslims. Large number of houses ... were searched and many arrests made. At the time of house searches and arrest big army and police demonstrations were held to create a sense of terror in the mind of the non-Muslims. A further attack came upon the non-Muslims from the side of the Muslim mob.... Cries of 'saboteurs', 'enemy agents', 'fifth-columnists', 'disloyal elements' etc. were raised by the Pakistani press and the responsible officials and non-official Muslim leaders almost everywhere in East Bengal. Before a year of the new state was completed, virtually a reign of terror was let loose upon the life of both the urban and rural non-Muslims by the police as well the officially inspired Muslim mob…. Government propaganda made the Muslim masses firmly suspicious that every Hindu in Pakistan was a fifth column of the Indian Union…. In many places, local boards and municipalities, having Hindu majorities, were arbitrarily suspended and their control taken over by the Government.

Guha lamented how Dhaka which was 'specially famous for its temples and Hindu festivals' was bereft of that festive fervour in just three years of Pakistan:

> To Vaishnavas, Dacca was second 'Brindaban'. A small city like Dacca contained as many as 700 Vaishnava temples along with many 'Kali temples' and some 'Gurdwaras'…. A large number of these temples have been destroyed, defiled or looted during the February riot. [1950] Some 26 important temples … are still under Muslim occupation. People of East Bengal, as of Dacca, are overwhelmingly Vaishnava…. Three years of Pakistan have made them so much terrorised, that while migrating to the Indian Union they have taken away with them 90 p.c. of their 'Vigrahas' and deities. Innumerable Hindu temples are still lying empty and vacant in the city of Dacca. (Ibid.)

The Janmashtami procession in Dhaka, which had been held for over 300 years and saw grand processions and lakhs of people congregate from various parts of East Bengal, Guha recorded, had to be abandoned in the very first year of Pak rule in East Bengal. Nearly forty-five *rathjatra*s, Guha recalled, 'used to come out in the streets' of Dhaka, but the February 1950 riots stopped all that; only a small procession took place that year in a village twenty miles from Dhaka. 'This, in a nutshell is the factual position of non-Muslims in

Dacca—a city which contained 58.5 p.c. Hindu population and whose predominance was manifest in every aspect of the city life—before partition,' Guha observed (Ibid.).

Guha's description of the gradual collapse of the Hindu social and religious fabric and ecosystem in East Bengal, post-partition, is vivid and continues to be unnerving. Narrated in a simple and yet moving manner, Guha's description of that collapse is worth narrating in some more detail:

> Trade and business of non-Muslims have almost collapsed.... Smiths, carpenters, fishermen, dhobis, milkmen and other non-Muslim classes belonging to similar other professions have migrated in very large numbers to the Indian Union. Barbers are now not easily available in East Bengal. Looking into the condition of East Bengal today one will feel as if the whole Hindu society has ceased to function there on its traditional system. The religious life of the Hindus is also on the verge of collapse. Temples and mandirs and maths and akharas, in overwhelming numbers are lying vacant. Sevayats and Sants have almost all migrated to India with their deities and vigrahas. In many cases, not only deities have been shifted to India but the buildings and properties of mandirs have been sold out to Muslims. In many more cases, vacant mandirs and temples are now being reduced to dwelling houses of Muslims. More than 85 p.c. of Hindu priests have migrated to India, even Sadhus, Sanths, Vaishnavas, Sannyasins and Jogis, who were known to have renounced their earthly life, have also migrated in very large numbers and [are] still migrating to Indian Union, leaving their ashrams, akharas, missions, devasthans, tirthas, kundas, etc. in conditions vacant and uncared for. (Ibid.)

And who were those 'unfortunate non-Muslims' who were still 'continuing their precarious existence in the fast-collapsing Hindu society of East Bengal today,' Guha said that they were the 'poorer section of the lower middle class, the peasantries, the agricultural labourers, the scheduled castes and other backward communities of Hindu society, who have neither means nor courage to dash for an unknown future in Indian Union'.

Samar Guha was not an 'RSS man', and therefore, his testimony may be more acceptable to those, especially the leftists and self-styled secularists, who opposed the CAA. But for convenience's sake, they preferred to suppress this dimension of Guha's life. They prefer to forget him, or at least this aspect of his life.

But not all communists were as devoid of conscience as the present breed of Indian communists. Let us start with the example of Comrade Bhupesh Gupta from Mymensingh, who was one of the intellectual and ideological icons of the left movement in India. At least on four occasions, Gupta, who was a member of the Rajya Sabha for decades, spoke on the refugees of East Pakistan.

On 4 March 1964, Gupta argued,

We are also committed to the minorities in Pakistan. We have signed the Nehru-Liaquat Pact … we cannot escape our responsibility in regard to this matter…. It seems since we signed the Nehru-Liaquat Pact, we went into some kind of sleep, became a little complacent…. But it was a mistake. We should have always taken up the cause of the minorities … especially when the agreement, which has some kind of international force, the Nehru-Liaquat Pact, was being violated by Pakistan, it was our duty to have informed the world public opinion through the diplomatic levels and otherwise.

The year 1964 saw another cycle of anti-Hindu pogrom in Pakistan. Hindus in East Pakistan bore the brunt. The present crop of communist leaders would be aghast at Gupta's proposition. They are used to complaining to the international community against India, against Narendra Modi and the BJP; they are the staunchest voices which speak for Pakistan on the international academic circuit!

Gupta again brought up the issue on 27 July 1970. He forcefully called on all to keep politics away for a while over this issue—of refugees, resettlement, and their rights. He argued,

> After all, those who are crossing into the frontier, they are not coming with political motives, they are not coming with the aim of supporting this or that party or opposing this party or that party, they are coming here because of certain fears and apprehensions there, they are coming here in quest of life, in order to get settlement and rehabilitation. Let us treat them in a spirit of brother taking brother and sister.

In 1974, Bhupesh Gupta's intervention on the issue was even more forceful. His line of argument was the same as that taken by Prime Minister Modi and Home Minister Amit Shah in December 2019 while placing the Citizenship Amendment Bill (CAB) in Parliament. Gupta's argument was also in line with the Jana Sangh's and later the BJP's argument on the need to fulfil our assurances given to the minorities in Pakistan at the time of partition.

Gupta noted how twenty-seven years had passed since the country was partitioned and asked the House to 'recall the speeches of the leaders of the Congress Party at that time, including in particular Jawaharlal Nehru's'. He said,

> At that time they gave clear assurance in their speeches, even before the country was partitioned, they would fully meet the aftermath of partition and that they will do everything in their power as the Government to resettle and rehabilitate the displaced persons from that part of Bengal which as a result of partition went to Pakistan. It was a solemn assurance which was repeated not only to outsiders or in press statements but also otherwise in many official statements of the Government of India.

Gupta insisted that it was 'necessary for the Government to give an explanation to the nation on why the assurances had been broken and how they came to be broken and who were responsible for it'.

Ironically, these are the same set of questions which the BJP asked of the Congress and the communist parties while they opposed the CAA. Ironically, Comrade Prakash Karat had written to the then Prime Minister Manmohan Singh, advocating the need to differentiate between those 'who have come to India due to economic reasons' and those people who had to 'flee their country in particular historical circumstances over which they had no control'. Karat had argued that the 'approach to granting citizenship to these unfortunate persons should be more liberal'. Karat's letter exposed communist hypocrisy. That the left is bereft of intellectual capital is evident from the manner in which they have jettisoned their past positions and the articulations of some of their leading lights.

Let us sample a few more, especially since the communist parties in West Bengal tried to outshout the Trinamool Congress (TMC) in their opposition to CAA. A number of CPI(M) MPs in the past supported the granting of citizenship and extensively quoted in Parliament the past promises made by Indian leaders. In a programme of the Matua community in December 2010, Gautam Deb, a senior leader of the CPI(M) and minister of housing and public health in the left government, spoke of the need to grant citizenship; he said that the government was bound to provide shelter to those minorities who were facing religious persecution in Bangladesh. The demand for granting citizenship was made in the rally, and it was supported by leaders of all parties present. Deb had shared the stage with state BJP leader Tathagata Roy and Manas Bhuniya, then West Bengal Pradesh Congress Committee (WBPCC) chief, who is now a TMC minister in West Bengal, and has been vocal in his opposition to CAA.

On 25 April 2012, Basudeb Acharia, one of the seniormost parliamentarians from the left and then Member of Parliament from Bankura in West Bengal, passionately raised the issue 'pertaining to lacs of people who came as refugees to our country from erstwhile Pakistan and Bangladesh because of their persecution as minorities'. These refugees 'have settled and are staying in different parts of the country and in different states like Uttarakhand, Uttar Pradesh, Madhya Pradesh, Chhattisgarh and Odisha', argued Acharia. 'They are staying in these States for years together. In spite of staying here for many years, these refugees have not been granted citizenship in our country.' Acharia reminded the then prime minister of his assurance: 'The granting of citizenship of these refugees would be considered favourably, but the Central Government, till today, have not considered granting citizenship to lacs of Bengali refugees.' Acharia, therefore, demanded that the 'Citizenship Act should be amended to grant citizenship to these Bengali refugees'.

Two other CPI(M) MPs, Shyamal Chakraborty and Prasanta Chatterjee, associated themselves with Acharia's demand. Chatterjee launched into a long-winded citation of the assurances given by leaders such as Mahatma Gandhi, Nehru, Sardar Patel, and others. Much in the same vein as Bhupesh Gupta decades earlier, Chatterjee reminded the House:

> When the country was partitioned, at that time there were some national commitments to the people who suffered because of this partition. Those commitments were made by no less persons like Mahatma Gandhi, Sri Jawaharlal Nehru and Sardar Vallabhbhai Patel. They guaranteed the security and safety of the people who were victims of the partition, that if they were forced to come over to this side of the subcontinent, you will be protected, you will be given shelter, you will be given food, and you will be given citizenship.

In 2012, the 20th Congress of the CPI(M) held at Kozhikode had called upon 'the Central Government to honour the assurance given by the Prime Minister to sympathetically consider the legitimate demand of the large numbers of Bengali refugees to recognise them as citizens of India. They had fled their country erstwhile East Pakistan and then Bangladesh.' The CPI(M) accepted that 'a large number of these refugees belong to the Scheduled Castes,

Namasudra communities and are living in different parts of the country'.

Adopting a perfidious stand today, the present stock of CPI(M) leaders thus have forsaken their past stance. They have vociferously opposed the CAA and were active in peddling a false narrative of fear and siege, especially among the Indian Muslims. In their opposition to the CAA, the Indian communists also clearly come across as anti-Bengali Hindu refugees.

At a time when the communist leaders are trying to keep themselves relevant by opposing the CAA, it is also necessary to remind them of their past record of massacring Bengali Hindu Dalit refugees who had taken shelter in the island of Marichjhapi in the estuary of Sunderban in 1979. It is a redeeming sign that the suppressed memory of that bloody episode is now resurfacing in the collective mind of West Bengal and the country as a whole.

It was a pogrom in which the communists can never be absolved of active complicity. It is a pogrom in which their complicity has been proved and documented and which remains unparalleled in the history of independent India. In the early years and decades after Independence, the communist party used the Bengali Hindu refugees as fodder for their political movements and protests, especially in West Bengal. Initially, the party refused to even ascertain or discuss the refugee problem. Between 1947 and 1948, issues of the communist weekly, *Peoples' Age* were strangely silent on this disturbing phenomenon. It was the period when communists had declared war on newly independent India. But gradually, they realized the potential that an organized refugee action could have on their own political growth and future in West Bengal.

A section of the refugees, having been promised by the communists that they would fight for their rights, threw their lots behind the communist parties. Having gradually propped themselves up on the shoulders and sweat of refugees, having promised them rehabilitation in West Bengal once they were in power, and having sent several feelers through leaders who repeatedly visited them, the communists conveniently forgot the refugees once they came to power in West Bengal in 1977. Ram Chatterjee, minister in the left front government in 1977, had repeatedly encouraged the refugees to come and settle in Sunderbans, which was a left stronghold. It is said,

> Having sold their belongings to pay for the trip, 15,000 refugee families left Dandakaranya only to discover that the Left Front policy had changed now that the coalition was in power, and many refugees were arrested and returned to the resettlement camps. The remaining refugees managed to slip through police cordons, reaching their objective of Marichjhapi island, where settlement began. By their own efforts they established a viable fishing industry, salt pans, a health centre, and schools over the following year.

This was anathema to the left government, especially to the CPI(M) and the CPI. They feared that this would lead to more refugees trickling in and would eventually upset the political equation. The communists feared these refugees would one day unseat them.

When these refugees, driven by that promise, began moving towards West Bengal and to settle in the far-off remote estuary island of Marichjhapi, they were fired upon and killed, their huts were burnt and their wells poisoned, and their children were drowned and starved by the CPI(M)-led left front government then headed by Comrade Jyoti Basu. The refugees did not want to be dependent on the government or survive on doles; all that they had asked for was a corner which they could call their own to start afresh and pick up the threads of their broken and shattered lives. Jyoti Basu's government launched an economic blockade on the settlement on 26 January 1979, 'with thirty police launches. The community was tear-gassed, huts were razed, and fisheries and tube wells were destroyed, in an attempt to deprive refugees of food and water'.

Instead of fulfilling its promise and commiserating with them, most of whom were Dalits, Comrade Jyoti Basu's government ordered them to be killed and thrown to the sharks. This is the reality of how Indian communists treated Bengali Hindu Dalit refugees in the past. When journalists began reporting the gory details of the Marichjhapi massacre, Basu promptly declared the area out of bounds for the media. The blockade led to starvation deaths and the left front government clamped Section 144, prohibiting movement; the refugees approached the Calcutta High Court which ruled 'against interference in the refugees' movements and their access to food and water. The government then denied that the refugees were subject to any blockade and continued the blockade in defiance of the High Court. Since the police union was under CPI (M) control, the court system had been effectively 'bypassed in this instance'. When the refugees persisted and the blockade failed,

the State Government ordered the forcible evacuation of the refugees, which took place from May 14 to May

16, 1979. Muslim gangs were hired to assist the police, as it was thought Muslims would be less sympathetic to refugees from Muslim-ruled Bangladesh. The men were first separated from the women. 'Most of the young men were arrested and sent to the jails and the police began to rape the helpless young women at random.'

Figures indicate that at least 17,000 people died in Marichjhapi and over 4,000 families died in transit out of exhaustion and starvation. An Indian administrative service officer in the rank of a secretary to the communist government of West Bengal who worked with ministers involved in the eviction confided to a leading researcher of the Marichjhapi massacre:

The bodies of the victims at Marichjhapi were dumped in the river to be washed out by the tide. This [made] the exhumation of bodies as was undertaken in Bosnia and Cambodia impossible, and in this macabre sense the refugees' selection of the Sundarbans was to prove not only unfortunate in their lives but in uncovering their deaths as well, since there were no human settlements downstream to observe the bodies.

Meanwhile, having executed the genocide, the 'CPM congratulated its participant members on their successful operation at Marichjhapi and made their refugee policy reversal explicit stating that "there was no possibility of giving shelter to these large number of refugees under any circumstances in the State"'. Eventually, the communists got away with this massacre of Bengali Dalit Hindu refugees, the worst in post-Independent India's history.

The communists have always stood by the illegal infiltrators while passing resolutions in support of refugees. But in reality, they have always opposed all attempts at conferring on them the possibilities of a dignified life and have instead sided with the politics of the vote-bank, in their case entirely based on the infiltrators. They have jettisoned the refugees who stood by them, spoke for them, and had fallen for their promises.

Their genocidal behaviour in Marichjhapi exposed their hypocrisy. 'Nowhere was the CPIM's switch of its role and policy on assuming power as sharp as on the issue of accepting the refugees of East Bengal,' writes Ross Mallick, a pioneering scholar on left rule in West Bengal. He argued that in the first Left Front government, the top-ranking 'CPM cabinet members were from East Bengal, including Jyoti Basu, Ashok Mitra, Prasanta Sur and Krishnapada Ghosh. The State Secretary Promode Das Gupta was also from East Bengal'. The CPI (M), Mallick pointed out, 'had built up its base in part through taking up the cause of the refugees and demanding that they be settled in West Bengal rather than dispersed throughout the country as was the Congress government policy'. Jyoti Basu had presented their case in the West Bengal Assembly in the 1950s and early 1960s during the B.C. Roy government. As late as December 1974 Jyoti Basu had demanded in a public meeting that the Dandakaranya refugees be allowed to settle in the Sunderbans. At a convention of eight 'Left Front Parties in 1975 it was resolved that the refugees be settled in the Sunderbans and a memorandum to that effect was proposed to be submitted to the Governor'. Never was a starker and bloodier volte-face seen as was in the case of the communists vis-à-vis the refugees of Marichjhapi, who faced the communist bludgeon as soon as the first Left Front government was formed, substantially due to their support and strength. In the annals of the history of independent India, this must surely go down as the darkest and bloodiest.

Through their opposition to the CAA, their outpouring of venom against it by passing resolutions and carrying on an international campaign of calumny against it, the communist and the left parties in India resorted to a second Marichjhapi; they are trying to crush the souls and aspirations of these refugees who have at last begun seeing a way out of an anonymous and uncertain existence because of the passage of the CAA.

This perfidious and duplicitous behaviour, this approach of trying to decimate the aspirations of these refugees, and the constant teaming up with the separatists' demand for India's dismemberment delineates the crisis of the left in India. In their self-consuming hatred for Narendra Modi, they have lost even the little sense of India they had perhaps once possessed. Their blind and irrational opposition to the CAA was a manifestation of that. It also announced its final unravelling.

7

Keeping the Promise

Struggle for Refugees and Citizenship over the Decades—RSS, Jana Sangh, BJP

In its 2019 Vision Document released during the election campaign, the Bharatiya Janata Party (BJP) clearly stated its intent of bringing about the Citizenship Amendment Bill. Since its founding, the Bharatiya Jana Sangh (BJS) and later the BJP have always advocated the need for providing citizenship to the beleaguered minorities of Pakistan, to protect them and to fulfil the promise India made to them at the time of partition. The Jana Sangh's first inaugural all-India session on 21 October 1951 under the presidency of Dr Syama Prasad Mookerjee spoke of giving 'top priority' to the 'problem of rehabilitation of displaced persons'.

For the Jana Sangh, the 'rehabilitation of those who have suffered from partition and come over to *Bharat* [was] legally as well as morally the responsibility of *Bharat* which must not be side-tracked'. In his presidential address at the first Annual Session of Jana Sangh in Kanpur in December 1952, Dr Mookerjee spoke of the need to form an 'independent commission to consider the nature and extent of rehabilitation' needed for refugees from both eastern and western Pakistan. Dr Mookerjee told the workers and leaders of the newly formed party:

> It is for the cause of India's freedom that millions of patriotic men and women had been sacrificed and had been treated in a brutal and inhuman fashion. If we fail to do justice to them and to their children, we will be committing an unforgivable sin for which we and our posterity will have to suffer.

The BJS's Kanpur session referred to the 'continuously deteriorating condition of the Hindus in East Bengal'; it pointed out how Pakistan's policy was to 'drive out all those who are of strong will and to force through atrocities the weaker to embrace Islam'. It reminded the ruling Congress party:

> The Hindus of Pakistan had not asked for partition but it was thrust upon them against their wishes and at the time of partition leaders of India including Mahatma Gandhi, Sardar Patel and Shri Nehru had given them the clear promise that it would be the duty of the people and the Government of India to always consider protection of their interests.

Of the fifteen resolutions passed by the Jana Sangh session in Kanpur, one spoke of 'rehabilitation' and detailed what needed to be done in order to expedite rehabilitation and compensation for the refugees from Pakistan.

Even after Dr Mookerjee's sudden death in Kashmir, when the fledgling BJS did not have the advantage of his leadership, under the tutelage of Pandit Deendayal

Upadhyaya, it kept up its support for Hindus of Pakistan and East Bengal. Following the footsteps of his leader Syama Prasad Mookerjee, Deendayal Upadhyaya spoke and wrote extensively on the issues of Hindu refugees and their displacement and rehabilitation. His interventions, therefore, did not allow the issue to sink as the Congress would have wanted it to.

Writing in *Panchajanya* in the first week of January 1952, just a few months after the Jana Sangh had been founded, Upadhyaya observed, referring to the Nehru–Liaquat Pact, that though 'every political party in India is committed to the protection of the four crore Muslims living in India, Pakistan had violated its part of the promise'. Upadhyaya argued that the atrocities committed on Hindus in eastern Bengal were 'ample evidence' of that fact. 'What is Nehru doing in this regard? Sardar Patel was not communal, but even he demanded half of East Bengal from Pakistan to house the displaced Hindus. Why does Nehru not raise this issue today?' he asked.

Addressing the press in Pune, in mid-November 1953, Upadhyaya said that the Jana Sangh was planning to launch a countrywide agitation 'to see that the interests of Hindus in Pakistan are safeguarded'. The *Times of India* reported that the 'agitation would be directed towards mobilising public opinion and influencing the Government of India to do all it could to ensure that the minorities in Pakistan got equal and honourable treatment'.

In its all-India session of August 1954 held at Indore, the BJS spoke of the problem of displaced persons as having two chief aspects: 'rehabilitation and compensation'. It argued that it was the Government of India's 'moral and legal responsibility to rehabilitate displaced persons and compensate them in full for losses suffered as a consequence of partition'.

The BJS central working committee meeting in Delhi in October 1955 expressed its deep concern 'over the increasing influx of Hindus from East Bengal. The hopes created by the formation of the non-Muslim League Ministry in East Bengal have been belied by the figures of the Hindu refugees coming from there during the recent months'. The BJS Central Working Committee (CWC) was referring to the very short-lived A.K. Fazlul Huq ministry in East Bengal which came to power for a month in 1954 before being dismissed by the West Pakistani Punjabi-dominated central government. It said, 'It has become clear that the plight of Hindus there continues to be precarious and that they have no alternative except to become converts to Islam or migrate to India sooner or later.' The BJS called upon the government to review its policy about East Bengal.

In its session in Gokak, Karnataka, in April 1955, the BJS CWC again took up the issue of the 'East Bengali Minorities' accusing Pakistan of its 'incapacity to protect life, honour and property of its minorities' and of deliberately strangulating 'their economic life with a view to squeezing them out of Pakistan'. It spoke of India's moral responsibility towards the minorities of East Bengal and a 'free East Bengal'. Expressing scepticism of the Karachi Agreement, which was an agreement on the transfer of evacuee bank accounts and transfer of lockers and safe deposits, the BJS CWC said a 'psychological atmosphere' for its success was necessary, and for that, BJS had a bold suggestion to the Congress: 'Men of influence in the social, economic and political spheres of East Bengal who have migrated to India must be persuaded to go back to their original homes in

East Bengal' and Congress leaders 'some of whom now hold power in West Bengal must give the lead in the matter. This fact more than anything else will restore confidence in Hindus still living in East Bengal'. If Nehru repeatedly asked the Bengali Hindus from East Bengal to return, why not start with Congressmen who had come away to West Bengal post-partition?

In its Kolkata session of 28 August 1955, the All-India General Council (AIGC) of BJS discussed in detail the plight of the Hindus of East Bengal. Describing the contrasting scenario in the western and eastern wings of Pakistan, its resolution noted that as far as the West Pakistan provinces were concerned 'practically the entire Hindu population there had to flee for their lives and come away due to the in-human atrocities perpetrated on them. As such, there has resulted an almost entire "Exchange of Population". No further exodus from West Pakistan is now taking place'. But the situation on the East Bengal front was different. In this area,

> there has been no such exchange of population. It has been really a one-way traffic—Hindus from East Bengal are coming away, but no Muslims of the (*Purbanchal*) Eastern zone (West Bengal, Assam, Bihar and Orissa) are leaving for East Bengal. In fact, in West Bengal itself some 50 lacs of Muslims are residing.

Describing the condition of the Bengali Hindus of East Pakistan, the BJS–AIGC resolution spoke of how they were 'oppressed and suppressed in a thousand ways', with their economic life being strangled, while their economic and cultural life is sought to be perverted. It accused the

Congress government of not facing these unpleasant facts and of trying to suppress them. Interestingly, the BJS meet at Kolkata not only spoke of the need to take adequate steps to 'rehabilitate the Hindu refugees from East Bengal' but also so that they could become 'economically self-supporting and stand upon their own legs and become useful members of society'; it also spoke of giving to the refugees from Pakistan 'full citizens' status in India automatically 'without the troublesome procedure of registration'.

Upadhyaya discussed Pakistan's New Islamic Constitution in the columns of *Panchajanya* on 23 January 1956. The new Islamic constitution of Pakistan, Upadhyaya observed, 'discriminates between Muslims and non-Muslims, and it is laid down that no non-Muslim can contest elections for the post of President or Vice President' and that 'Islamic ideals and code of conduct will be applicable to both the country's leaders and government'. Of the future of Hindus in Pakistan, Upadhyaya wrote, rightly analysing the Pakistan establishment's ruse:

> Despite the population of East Pakistan being more than double of that of West Pakistan, the constitution attempts to place both on par without taking this fact into account. This part of the Pakistani constitution is wholly unjust and a treacherous attempt to destroy the Hindu influence on the social life and activity of East Pakistan. Pakistani leaders are not prepared to give equal rights to Hindus. They also know very well that despite being the majority, the Muslims of East Pakistan follow the traditional Hindu way of life. The Muslims of that part of the subcontinent, under the influence of the anti-Hindu propaganda and malicious feelings of the Muslim League, may have fallen for its bogus ideas, but once the reaction dies down, they will feel

that Urdu and Arabic are foreign (unfamiliar) languages for them and they are close to the Bengali language. This constitution wishes to impose Islamic culture on the people of East Bengal. (2019)

Years before the Bangladesh Liberation War, Upadhyaya had rightly assessed the forces and currents at work which would eventually push the eastern wing of Pakistan to break away and form Bangladesh in 1971. The constitution changed the name of East Bengal to East Pakistan because, Upadhyaya argued, 'Pakistan knows that East Bengal is Bengal first and Pakistan only after that. The principle of equality works against the Hindus of East Bengal because of their majority there and is meant to reduce their influence' (ibid.). The Hindus in Pakistan were being subjected to boycott as second-class citizens and it was 'impossible for them to live with any dignity in Pakistan' with more than a crore of Hindus having already migrated to India. 'More than 20,000 people are crossing the border every month,' Upadhyaya wrote, 'and with the passing of this constitution the future of the minority community in Pakistan will be dark' (ibid.). Upadhyaya called upon the Nehru dispensation to 'pay attention to these patently unfair and discriminatory sections of Pakistan's constitution'. It was not correct to say that it was an internal matter of Pakistan. He said:

> The fate of Hindus of Pakistan is closely linked to us. Our duty lies in not merely safeguarding the rights of Hindus but also in ensuring that a feeling of insecurity does not get entrenched in their hearts. Any intimidatory change compels them to leave their homes and come to India.

In April 1956, in the pages of *Panchajanya*, Upadhyaya again called for demanding land from Pakistan for the resettlement of the displaced people from East Pakistan. Upadhyaya assailed the Nehru government for practically stating that it would be unable 'to alleviate the sufferings of its children'. What about 'those assurances which our leaders had doled out to the Hindus of East Bengal at the time of Partition? They had then accepted the responsibility of ensuring fair treatment to minorities in Pakistan,' he said. Speaking of the Nehru–Liaquat Pact of 1950, Upadhyaya wrote that it was 'not even worth the paper' it was written on. Recalling Sardar Patel's demand of land from Pakistan for those minorities it had evicted, Upadhyaya castigated the Congress government for not only not taking any steps, but, on the contrary, for having appallingly decided to 'seal the borders to keep out those who flee Pakistan'. This decision of the government 'had badly hurt the sentiments of all nationalist-minded people,' he said. Upadhyaya also pointed at the irony of the decision, since a few months earlier, the Pakistan High Commissioner to India had himself made a similar suggestion. 'Instead of rescuing those who are being hunted,' Upadhyaya observed, the Nehru government was:

closing its own doors on those unfortunate souls, so that they are left to their fate and suffer. If the Pakistan regime is responsible for forced conversions and atrocities on Hindus, the Government of India is guilty of shrouding this crime and making it even more complicated. Sealing the borders might stop the flow of refugees into India but the fate of our brothers and sisters living in Pakistan will only worsen. We can imagine what they undergo as they sell off even their homes and property and reach Dhaka to obtain papers in the hope of reaching a country where they feel they will be treated and respected like other Hindus. But the doors of our Deputy High Commissioner are closed to them.

The BJS's All-India meet in Jaipur towards the end of April 1956 expressed profound shock at the Congress government's reversal of policy towards Hindus from East Bengal by restricting the issuance of certificates to 'intending Hindu migrants who had to leave their hearths and homes in East Bengal in view of the intolerable conditions prevailing there for the Hindu minorities, particularly after the declaration of Pakistan as an Islamic Republic'. This restriction, the BJS argued, has 'virtually amounted to "banning" further the migration from Pakistan to India' of the minorities. This banning, thus, was, according to them:

> gross violation of the basic conditions of the partition of India, i.e., the minorities must be assured honourable existence, with absolute security of life, property and equality of opportunities for livelihood and failing which, the minorities must have the freedom to migrate.

Condemning the weak-kneed policy of the Government of India, the BJS called for 'reciprocity' in relations with Pakistan or 'exchange of population', and 'demanding additional territory from Pakistan to accommodate the teeming millions of Hindu migrants'. It also cautioned the Nehru government that it must not be under the illusion that 'migration is going to cease or that it is only temporary and that the migrants may even possibly return to Pakistan and so on' but must instead proceed on the basis that someday if the present conditions continued, the entire Hindu population of Pakistan may come over to India. The government therefore needed to make provisions for that massive eventuality.

The BJS's manifesto for the 1957 general elections spoke of the 'exodus of Hindus from East Bengal'. The Jana Sangh manifesto spoke of how the 'Congress Government which was pledged to protect the life and property of Hindus in East Bengal' had failed to live up to its promise. It argued that 'no Hindu could live with honour in East Bengal' and promised to 'mobilise world public opinion against the forcible squeezing out of Hindus from East Bengal' and to demand 'land from Pakistan for resettling' Hindus being driven out of East Bengal. It argued that no 'restrictions, direct or indirect' could be placed 'on granting visas to those Hindus in East Bengal who are desirous of migrating to India' and called for 'full facilities to those who have anyhow crossed the border and come to *Bharat*'.

Meeting in Bilaspur in August 1957, the BJS's AIGC reminded the Nehru dispensation of the solemn assurances given at the time of partition by 'authorities on either side, that the minorities in either State would be accorded full rights of citizenship and their lives and properties and honour would be ensured' and that if these conditions were not fulfilled, 'the minorities were, if they so desired, free to migrate without any restrictions and that the full responsibility for their resettlement and rehabilitation would be with the State to which they migrated'. That was how the BJS's resolution recalled the 'fundamental basis of the partition arrangement'. It described the Nehru government's move to restrict migration certificates as 'callous, heartless and disgraceful' followed by 'utter violation of its solemn pledges to the minorities in Pakistan given at the time of partition'. The situation led 'lacs of Hindus who sold out all their possessions in East Bengal because of their decision to come over to the Indian Union' to being stranded.

The BJS's CWC meet in Hyderabad in November 1957 discussed the conditions of refugees and their rehabilitation. It spoke of the large number of pending requests for migration certificates, of incomplete rehabilitation measures for refugees from Pakistan, of the need for demanding 'adequate territory from East Bengal to settle the Hindu migrants from there' and of the abolition of the 'passport-cum-visa system' so that Hindus who wish to come to India can easily do so.

In 1958, the Central Working Committee (CWC) of the Jana Sangh, meeting in Mumbai in July, condemned the government's decision to close down refugee camps in West Bengal and shift the bulk of their inmates 'to distant areas outside Bengal' and that those who declined to shift out to other locations would be 'given a small lump sum and then left to their own fate'. This, the Jana Sangh CWC argued, 'will only aggravate the unemployment problem in West Bengal' and is 'callous and inhuman' and 'goes directly against the Government assurances held out after the last Refugee *Satyagraha* in West Bengal that no refugee would be shifted outside Bengal against his will'.

In its manifesto of 1962, the Jana Sangh called for rehabilitating displaced persons from East Pakistan in areas that were 'congenial to them' and spoke of their right to full compensation. It also spoke of a speedy completion of the Dandakaranya refugee rehabilitation project. Meeting in May 1962 in Kota, Rajasthan, the BJS's AIGC again passed a resolution on the East Bengali minorities.

It spoke of the 'widespread atrocities against Hindus in East Bengal' which were not just sporadic events but were the 'result of a deep-laid conspiracy to which the highest officials in Pakistan have been a party'. It spoke of the vitriol poured on the Hindus by General Ayub Khan and the East Bengal governor and of the 'spate of murder, arson and plundering let loose against Hindus in East Bengal'. It was evident that the Hindus in Pakistan 'had become veritable hostages in the hands of the Government there'. The BJS meet reiterated its demand for territory and compensation from Pakistan to rehabilitate Hindus who remained in Pakistan.

In a column in the *Organiser* issue of 3 February 1964, entitled, 'Kashmir and East Bengal: Things have gone too far and gone on much too long', Deendayal Upadhyaya argued that Pakistan's attempt to refer the Kashmir issue to the United Nations Security Council (UNSC) was 'mainly to divert attention of the world from its criminal activities in East Bengal' where there is 'no security of life and property for the Hindus'. The unending stream of refugees had swelled to 50,00,000, and to:

> say that the Government of Pakistan failed to protect them is to take away [from] that Islamic Government the credit for implementing its plans of *Jihad*. The Government of Pakistan has been a party to all these heinous crimes. In a planned manner it has been squeezing out the Hindus from Pakistan and it will continue to do so till the last Hindu has been done with. In the land of Islam i.e. Dar-ul-Islam, there is no room for a *kafir*.

Raising a hue and cry over Kashmir at the UNSC was therefore a clever ploy by Pakistan 'to put world opinion off the scent' of the atrocities being committed on Hindus in East Pakistan.

In another of his columns in the *Organiser*, writing on 21 June 1965, Deendayal Upadhyaya, welcoming the decision of the state Home Ministers' conference to 'hand over the policing of the borders to centre', called for clearing a 10-mile belt along the border of anti-India and pro-Pak elements for settling displaced people from East Bengal in these areas. Upadhyaya foresaw a 'fresh wave of communal frenzy and mass exodus of Hindus to India' from East Bengal because of the conditions of insecurity that Pakistan continued to create there. He wrote,

> The Government of India should give a clear warning to the Government of Pakistan that it shall no longer be a passive spectator of any crimes against the Hindus in East Bengal and instead of receiving the migrants, it shall be constrained to resort to 'police action' in the solemn discharge of its obligations.

The Jana Sangh's manifesto for the 1967 general elections spoke of a 'continuous exodus of non-Muslims, particularly Hindus, from Pakistan due to its anti-Hindu policy and occasional programmes of squeezing them out by inciting large-scale riots'. It spoke of how 'one crore people have migrated to India' and the government has not done much in rehabilitating them. The BJS pledged to confer on them citizenship rights in the course of rehabilitation. The demand, for conferring citizenship rights, thus is an old promise made by the BJP's political predecessor, the Jana Sangh, which continued to be upheld by the BJP. It was fulfilled the moment an opportunity arose. Just because the Congress and communist parties did not read or did not know of the details of the BJS's history and the BJP's promises, they think it is a new-fangled idea implemented to create unrest and to firm up the vote bank in the country by the BJP.

In the crucial year of 1971, the Jana Sangh continued to highlight how, after more than two decades, 'lakhs of refugees continue to pour in from East Pakistan year after year' and are living in 'shocking conditions'. It promised, among other things, 'to expedite the rehabilitation of refugees already' in India.

Atal Bihari Vajpayee, in Parliament, forcefully intervened to repeatedly articulate the Jana Sangh's line on Bangladesh. In its Udaipur all-India session in July 1971, the BJS strongly advocated for the recognition of *Swadhin Bangladesh*— independent Bangladesh. Terming Pakistan as a 'monstrous absurdity', the BJS session argued,

> Philosophy or ideology which assumed that Dacca [sic] could feel itself closer to Lahore and Islamabad—some 1200 miles away than to Calcutta [sic] and that a citizen of East Bengal could find greater affinity with a citizen of West Punjab than with his next door non-Muslim Bengali neighbour is as preposterous as it is illogical, unscientific and unrealistic.

It then proposed various steps to render support to the demand for Bangladesh and the need to recognize it. The Jana Sangh mobilized public opinion through countrywide movements in support of the Bangladesh liberation movement and was the first political party to repeatedly demand that Bangladesh be recognized and that a firm line be taken with Pakistan. Atal Bihari Vajpayee's interventions in Parliament throughout 1971 give an idea of Jana Sangh's political stand and its policy towards these momentous events. Speaking on the 'holocaust in Bangladesh' and of 'liberation as the only solution', Vajpayee spoke of how 'since the partition of the country one crore eighty lakh people have come to India from East Bengal' and of people having been 'slaughtered on a mass scale' and of fields having been destroyed, of houses burnt:

> Young girls have been gang-raped. Small children were flung in the air and caught on bayonet points. So long as Pakistan that has committed such sins remains there, can any displaced person return? Nobody will go back and we can only imagine what will happen to this country.

The need to effectively rehabilitate Bengali Hindu refugees and other minorities from East Bengal and the conferring of citizenship rights on minorities from Pakistan was an issue that would become one of the core demands of Jana Sangh over the decades. This detailed look at some of its resolutions is to reiterate the point that the Jana Sangh never failed to stick to it—it never backtracked and fell short in highlighting it.

The cause of the refugees and the need to grant them citizenship was continuously referred to through party programmes, resolutions in the party's meetings, and by the party's leaders in the Parliament. Deendayal Upadhyaya himself wrote extensively and prolifically on the issue, while leaders like Atal Bihari Vajpayee kept it alive, for decades, within the legislature. It was a fundamental demand which, with a few others, shaped its politics over the decades. It was the Jana Sangh and later the BJP, among political parties, which kept up the struggle for rehabilitation and citizenship. Syama Prasad Mookerjee's resignation from the Nehru cabinet in April 1950 was on the issue of Nehru's inability or unwillingness to provide the promised protection to the Hindus of East Bengal who were facing persecution. The Jana Sangh therefore never allowed that issue to recede into the background.

At the forefront of rescuing Hindu refugees during partition, the Rashtriya Swayamsevak Sangh (RSS) took up the issue of beleaguered Hindus of East Bengal and of those among them who had come over to West Bengal. Sri Guruji Golwalkar, RSS Sarsanghchalak, in tours across India and especially in the northern provinces and West Bengal, was deeply hurt by the condition of the refugees, especially in West Bengal. Overnight, those Hindus who were left behind in East Pakistan had become aliens and foreign refugees. Sri Guruji did not want to depend on governmental support alone to provide relief to these Hindu refugees.

In order to mobilize and garner people's support, the *Vastuhara Sahayata Samiti* was set up by the RSS in Kolkata on 8 February 1950, and Sri Guruji, on reaching Delhi, issued 'an appeal to the nation describing the plight of Hindus in East Pakistan and urging people to come forward to help generously' for their relief. The Sangh's work in West Bengal, Assam, and Odisha was still on a limited scale and Sri Guruji, in trying to broad-base the effort also appealed to the government to give up its indecision. He said,

If indecision, confused mindset and weakness of mind continue the Government of Bharat will be committing the grave sin of putting out the lives of crores of their innocent fellow-countrymen. Its reputation will bite dust. So, the need is to act fearlessly, without getting mired in a senseless discussion of communalism, and do the needful, whether it is police action [against East Pakistan in order to stop the pogroms against its minorities] or exchange of Hindus and Muslims. A plan for a proportional exchange of Hindus and Muslims left over in Bharat should be put into action immediately, so that our one-and-a-half crore brethren could be saved and could be made to lead a life of peace, honour and happiness.

Sri Guruji also appealed to everyone, during these surcharged days, to 'express their anguish in a controlled manner' and 'avoid activities that may disturb peace and create hindrances in the way of the Government. We must beware of indulging in any antisocial, anti-national and undesirable actions,' he urged. The RSS set up an independent centre of relief for the refugees and also called for support from the government in any effort it was making to provide relief to the refugees from East Bengal. Sri Guruji's appeal had its desired effect, and help for Hindu refugees from East Bengal began pouring in. Led by a team of dedicated *swayamsevak*s, the *Vastuhara Sahayata Samiti* expanded its work. The orgies of violence in East Bengal continued unabated for a full year, increasing the refugee influx, the Samiti diversified its relief work to providing shelter, medical help, and helping them get employment; special schools were opened for the refugee children and more than 80,000 refugees were catered to, while a few lakhs more given food grains and clothes. A team of 5,000 *swayamsevak*s worked round the clock for over a year till the wave had mitigated somewhat. In the meantime, Sri Guruji was being consulted by Sardar Patel, and he kept his channels of communication open. The growing refugee influx from East Pakistan was generating severe reactions across the country. Sri Guruji wrote to Sardar Patel on 5 April 1950, 'We are aware that it would be highly improper to exploit the situation which would endanger peace or incite feelings against the government. We believe in maintaining peace, and it is in this attitude that we are serving the sufferers.' Sri Guruji met Sardar Patel in Delhi on 22 April 1950 and apprised him of the extensive relief operations carried out by the Sahayata Samiti. Sardar Patel was very pleased with the effort and urged Sri Guruji to rapidly expand the Sangh's work in the eastern parts of India. Contrary to a false miasma created by false narratives peddled by the Congress and the communists, the RSS was at the forefront of refugee relief and rehabilitation and played a crucial role in providing succour and relief to the Bengali Hindu refugees from East Bengal. This is a dimension of history that has been conveniently forgotten or marginalized.

From the 1960s onwards, the RSS's national meets have consistently dwelt on the plight of the minorities in Pakistan, especially in East Pakistan. Each major pogrom on Hindus in East Bengal, East Pakistan, and later in Bangladesh—especially in 1978, 1993, 1994, and 2021 saw the RSS call for strong measures for relief, rehabilitation of refugees, and strong and decisive action by the Government of India to prevent anti-Hindu pogroms from occurring in future.

Supporting the CAA in 2019, then RSS Sarkaryavah Bhaiyya Ji Joshi said that it fulfilled a long-held hope and addressed a crucial issue that had been left unaddressed all these years. He said,

When the country was partitioned, there was a demand for division on religious grounds. However, India did not have any such idea of forming a 'religious country'. But the country was partitioned over this issue and the leaders then had accepted it. Subsequently, Pakistan and Bangladesh declared themselves as Islamic states and there were doubts then about what place the minorities residing there will get ... the Hindus residing there in large numbers became target of persecution. The question arises where these people went, and it comes to fore that many of them came to India. However, due to lack of provisions in the law, these people were deprived of the citizenship of India for many years.

Articulating the RSS's long-held view that 'these persecuted people may not be called "intruders", but termed as refugees', Bhaiyya Ji Joshi argued,

There is a need for these refugees to have a respectable life and common rights in our country. But a lot of time passed and these refugees had to wait. I feel this Bill [CAA] has assured the minorities coming from these countries, and we welcome them and express our happiness for them. Now, their refugee status will end and they will live as citizens and will get benefits of the citizens' rights.

Being the largest cultural non-governmental organisation in the world with a multi-dimensional social, educational, and service outreach, the RSS has largely kept alive the plight of the Bengali Hindus in East Pakistan then and Bangladesh later in the national discourse.

While most kept silent and looked the other way or were busy denying or disowning the Bengali Hindu refugees, the RSS, the Jana Sangh, and later the BJP steadfastly stood by them throughout the decades after Independence and partition. The passing of the CAA in 2019, thus, was a logical finale to those years of struggle and of humanitarian advocacy and of trying to remind us of all the promises made to the Hindus of Pakistan at the time of Independence.

Postscript

The CAA was notified by the Union home ministry on 11 March 2024. With the promulgation of the law, Prime Minister Narendra Modi fulfilled a promise he and his party had made for decades.

Despite their best attempts, the Congress, Indian Union Muslim League, Trinamool Congress and a bunch of Left-communist affiliated organisations could not prevent its implementation. The Supreme Court refused to stay the implementation of the CAA. These parties argued that Rohingyas and other infiltrators must also be given citizenship. The CAA, they said, was discriminatory in nature since it spoke of granting citizenship to adherents of particular communities persecuted on the basis of religion.

Simply put, these parties had a problem with and opposed the fact that the CAA spoke for the persecuted Hindus who lived as minorities in India's neighbouring countries. The CAA, to be sure, not only spoke for the persecuted Hindus but also extended this provision to persecuted Sikhs, Jains, Parsis and Christians from India's neighbourhood.

In May 2024, the first batch of fourteen applicants were conferred citizenship certificates under the CAA by the Union home secretary. It was an epochal milestone achieved after a long and arduous struggle for citizenship, rehabilitation, and dignity. The BJP under Narendra Modi had fulfilled one more of its foundational promises. It had not back peddled or prevaricated, rather it had acted boldly, sagaciously withstanding the calculated onslaught of false narratives and propaganda, engineered riots and disturbances, to achieve a promise that was made by the founding leaders of the Indian republic but forsaken over the years.

It was indeed a long struggle since independence, and from 1971 onwards, when another tectonic displacement had taken place. Speaking of the persecution of Hindus and their displacement in 1971 from East Bengal by the Pakistani establishment and army, Richard Pilkington, scholar of genocide studies, in his seminal *The West and the Birth of Bangladesh: Foreign Policy in the Face of Mass Atrocity* writes, 'The systematic persecution of Hindus in East Bengal created one of the greatest exoduses of refugees in modern history. By mid-July [1971], some seven million people had flooded into the sensitive areas of northern India and beyond in pursuit of safety. Despite the fact that Hindus represented only 15 percent of the population of East Pakistan, they formed the clear majority in the camps.' Political parties and non-political forums that opposed the CAA and rushed to the Supreme Court in an attempt to stymie its implementation wanted us to forget this unnerving and gory past.

Not many remember that in the first few years after independence Dr Syama Prasad Mookerjee exerted himself for the rehabilitation of refugees, besides exposing Pakistan and the Nehru-led Congress in the manner in which they treated the Bengali Hindus of East Bengal.

As president of the Bengal Rehabilitation Organisation, Dr Mookerjee formed the Bengal Rehabilitation Board and invited the leading sociologist Dr Radhakamal Mukherjee, a close colleague, to head it as the chairman.

The board came out with an exhaustive report on refugee rehabilitation. The report argued that the 'main objectives of refugee rehabilitation' were 'the planned utilization, development and redistribution of man-power so as to (a) restore the economic and social life of the displaced community and (b) reconstruct the economic life of West Bengal'. It argued that refugee rehabilitation 'scientifically planned and implemented' could give 'a new lease of life to the decadent, truncated state'. The report proffered suggestions and a roadmap for refugee rehabilitation and also drew up a detailed plan on how the 'economy of West Bengal could be so organized and developed that both the refugees and original inhabitants of West Bengal' might benefit, 'signaling an overall prosperity of the State'.

As early as September 1947, the RSS spoke of the need for a plan for refugee rehabilitation. A number of pieces in the *Organiser* not only highlighted the conditions of the displaced Hindus from Pakistan but also spoke of the need to make 'arrangements to settle the refugees in life'. These pieces talked about 'starting cottage industries on a cooperative basis and teaching handicrafts which can be picked up … such as lock making, tailoring, weaving, knitting and hand-embroidery, basket-making, shoe-making etc.' and went on to list several initiatives that needed to be launched to enable this to happen.

While Nehru refused rehabilitation to the refugees from East Bengal whom he abused, Syama Prasad Mookerjee and the RSS not only worked to ensure relief for refugees but also planned, ideated, and provided roadmaps for free India to address this mammoth problem.

I write about these in a postscript to emphasise the point that refugee rehabilitation, citizenship, and dignity are issues that were fundamental to the belief, ideology, and philosophy of the RSS, the Jana Sangh, and later to the BJP. They were the ones who continually spoke up on the plight of the Hindus from East Bengal, while most others preferred to keep silent or to ignore them. They kept silent so that the saga of their grievous and erroneous handling of refugees from East Bengal could be suppressed and eventually obliterated from our collective memory.

Such obfuscators of history also opposed Narendra Modi, when in 2022 he spoke of declaring 14 August as a day of remembering those who suffered the torments of partition and perished. They opposed the naming of the day as 'Partition Horrors Remembrance Day'. Why should the tragedy of partition be recalled and remembered? some of them argued. Those who argued thus belonged to a political ideology and lineage that had a history of prejudice and bias against refugees and persecuted minorities of East Bengal. Modi's call was not a partisan one. He spoke of the need for a free nation to remember those who suffered the effects of partition, those who could not live in a free India, those who faced displacement and decimation, and those whose future were snatched away. They found fault even in that call, which came across as deeply uncomfortable given the bitter truths of history. In their opposition to the CAA, they were driven by the same ingrained prejudice and motive. Yet people, including scholars, responded to Modi's call for 'Partition Horrors Remembrance Day' with the descendants of the affected people finding a sense of fulfilment.

This book is a response to those narrative setters who had hurled calumnies at the CAA and its raison-d'être and laboured to erase the story of the displaced Bengali

Hindus from East Bengal. It is a riposte to those ideological gatekeepers of history who have tried to draw the curtains on the story and history of persecuted minorities in India's neighbourhood and to those apologists who justify the flawed policies and politics of citizenship and rehabilitation undertaken by Nehru, his Congress and his drum beaters, the Indian communists. Together, they decided and shaped a number of India's decades after independence. Today, they would want the history of their deceitful conduct to sink into the dark nether of forgetfulness. It is that which needs to be resisted.

Acknowledgements

I am grateful to Praveen Tiwari, publishing director at BluOne Ink, for pushing me into bringing these writings together and to rewrite them in a book form. My thanks are also due to Thanglenhao Haokip, senior editor at BluOne Ink, for continuously pursuing me with his reminders and deadlines. I would be ungrateful if I do not mention my friend Anant Vijay, journalist and author, who regularly discussed ideas and repeatedly followed up on whether I was writing. The Prime Ministers Museum and Library are a mine of information on this phase of history and house a vast collection of Dr Mookerjee's papers; I am grateful for being able to access this collection over the years, some of which have been essential for this book. I thank Dr Shailendra Shukla, research scholar at Dr Syama Prasad Mookerjee Research Foundation (SPMRF), for helping me sift through this wide array of material and for flagging the right material and documents. I am grateful to Ayush Anand, advocate-on-record at the Supreme Court, for helping me with various aspects on the CAA. I am also grateful to Prafull Ketkar, the editor of *Organiser*, for readily supplying me with material from the weekly's archives pertaining to the period immediately after the partition. Last but not the least, I thank my wife, Ms Anuttama Ganguly, secretary, Vivekananda International Foundation (VIF), for her unstinting support and encouragement while I persisted with my writing.

References

Prefatory Thoughts

Constituent Assembly Debates, 11 and 12 August 1949.

'Discussion on the Motion Regarding the Bengal Situation', 7 August 1950, Parliament, Second Session of the Parliament of India, *Parliamentary Debates,* 4 August 1950.

Naba Kumar Adak. *Syama Prasad Mookerjee: A Study of His Role in Bengal Politics* (1929–1953). New Delhi: Kunal Books, 2013.

Sri Aurobindo: Autobiographical Notes and Other Writings of Historical Interest. Puducherry: Sri Aurobindo Ashram Publication Dept, 2006.

Chapter 1: Pak Army Genocide and Exodus of Hindus in 1971: An Overlooked Chapter

Anirban Ganguly. 'Jana Sangh and Swadheen Bangladesh'. *Millennium Post*, 21 December 2021.

D.R. Mankekar. *Recurrent Exodus of Minorities from East Pakistan and Disturbances in India: A Report to the Indian Commission of Jurists by Its Committee of Enquiry.* New Delhi: The Indian Commission of Jurists, 1965.

———. *Pak Colonialism in East Bengal.* New Delhi: Somaiya Publications.

Farahnaz Ispahani. 2015. *Purifying the Land of the Pure: Pakistan's Religious Minorities.* Noida: Harper Collins India, 1971.

Gary J. Bass. *The Blood Telegram: India's Secret War in East Pakistan.* Noida: Random House India, 2013.

M.N. Ghatate, ed. *Atal Bihari Vajpayee: Four Decades in Parliament*, Vol. 3. New Delhi: Shipra Publications, 1996.

Martin Sokefeld. 1996. 'Teaching the Value of Nation and Islam in Pakistani Textbooks'. *Internationale Schulbuchforschung*, 18 (3): 289–306.

Narendra Modi. 'In the Last Few Years, India and Bangladesh have Written a Golden Chapter in Bilateral Ties: PM'. Full text of PM Narendra Modi's address available at: https://www.narendramodi. in/prime-minister-narendra-modi-s-video-message-to-bangladesh-on-100th-birth-anniversary-celebrations-of-bangabandhu-sheikh-mujibur-rahman--548825 (accessed on 19 March 2020).

P.N. Dhar. *Indira Gandhi: The 'Emergency' and Indian Democracy*. New Delhi: Oxford University Press, 2000.

P.N. Luthra. 'Problems of Refugees from East Pakistan'. *Economic and Political Weekly*, 6 (50) (11 December 1971): 2467–72.

Pravash Chandra Lahiry. 1964. *India Partitioned and Minorities in Pakistan*. Kolkata: Writers' Forum Pvt Ltd.

Sydney Schanberg. 'East Pakistani Town in Guerrilla Enclave Is Coming Back to Life'. *New York Times*.

———. 'Hindus are Target of Army Terror in an East Pakistan Town'. *New York Times*.

———. 'West Pakistan Pursues Subjugation of Bengalis'. *New York Times*.

———. 'Bengali Refugees Say Soldiers Continue to Kill, Loot and Burn'. *New York Times*, 21 September 1971.

Yvette Claire Rosser. 2003. *Curriculum as Destiny: Forging National Identity in India, Pakistan and Bangladesh*. Texas: University of Texas at Austin.

Chapter 2: 'We Will All Sink': How Nehru Duped Bengali Hindu Refugees

A.J. Kamra. *The Prolonged Partition and Its Pogroms: Testimonies on Violence against Hindus in East Bengal* 1946–64. New Delhi: Voice of India, 2000.

Amritlal Chattopadhyay. Presidential Address, North Kolkata East Bengal Refugee Convention, 30 October 1949, Dr Syama Prasad Mookerjee Papers. New Delhi: Prime Ministers' Museum and Library.

Parliamentary Debates, 17 March 1950.

Prafulla Chakrabarti. *The Marginal Men: The Refugees and the Left Political Syndrome in West Bengal*. Kolkata: Naya Udyog, 1999.

Rammanohar Lohia. *Guilty Men of India's Partition* (1960). New Delhi: B.R. Publishing Corporation, 2000.

Chapter 3: Congress's Doublespeak on and Neglect of Refugees from East Bengal

'*Recurrent Exodus of Minorities from East Pakistan and Disturbances in India*'. A Report to The Indian Commission of Jurists by its Committee of Enquiry, New Delhi: The Indian Commission of Jurists, 1965.

Dr Syama Prasad Mookerjee. 7 August 1950, Debate in Parliament on the Bengal Situation, 7 August 1950.

Prafulla Chakrabarti. 1999. *Marginal Men: The Refugees and the Left Political Syndrome in West Bengal*. Kolkata: Naya Udyog, 1999.

Pravash Chandra Lahiry. 1964. *India Partitioned and Minorities in Pakistan*. Kolkata: Writers' Forum Pvt. Ltd, 1964.

Voice of New India. *A Tale of Woes of East Pakistan Minorities*. Kolkata: D.R. Sen, 1966. 'Recurrent Exodus of Minorities from East Pakistan and Disturbances in India'

Chapter 4: Dalits and the Demand for a Bengali Hindu Homeland and Their Persecution in Islamic Pakistan

'Should Bengal Be Divided into Two Provinces', Statement Issued by Dr Syama Prasad Mookerjee, 19 March 1947. Kolkata: H.C. Ghose, Hindu Mahasabha.

A.J. Kamra. 2000. *The Prolonged Partition and Its Pogroms: Testimonies on Violence against Hindus in East Bengal 1946–64*. New Delhi: Voice of India, 2000.

Durga Das, ed. 1974. *Sardar Patel's Correspondence: 1945–1950*, vol. 10. Ahmedabad: Navajivan Publishing House, 1974.

Jogendra Nath Mandal's Resignation Letter of 9 October 1950. Reissued by Dr Syama Prasad Mookerjee Research Foundation, New Delhi, 2020.

Samar Guha. 1964. *Non-Muslims Behind the Curtain of East Pakistan.* Dhaka: East Bengal Minorities Association, 1964.

Sekhar Bandyopadhyay and Anasua Basu Ray Chaudhuri. 2022. *Caste and Partition in Bengal: The Story of Dalit Refugees, 1946–1961.* New Delhi: Oxford University Press, 2022.

Dhananjay Keer. 2016 (1954). *Dr Babasaheb Ambedkar: Life & Mission.* Mumbai: Popular Prakashan, 5th edition.

Ross Mallick. 1999. 'Refugee Resettlement in Forest Reserves: West Bengal Policy Reversal and the Marichjhapi Massacre'. *The Journal of Asian Studies*, 58 (1) (Feb).

Nitish Sengupta. 2012 (2007). *Bengal Divided: the Unmaking of a Nation – 1905–1971.* New Delhi: Penguin Books.

Dinesh Chandra Sinha. 2023. *Syama Prasad: Bangabibhag O Paschimbanga.* Kolkata: Tuhina Prakashani, reprint.

Chapter 5: On CAA the Congress Peddled False Narrative, Spread Misinformation, Betrayed Refugees, and Looked the Other Way

Amalendu Misra. 'Life in Brackets: Minority Christians and Hegemonic Violence in Pakistan', *International Journal on Minority and Group Rights*, Vol.22, No.2, 2015, pp. 157–181.

Bharatiya Jana Sangh. 'Policies and Manifestoes'. In *Party Documents: (1952–1980)*, vol.1. New Delhi: Bharatiya Janata Party, 2005.

Bharatiya Janata Party. 'Ek Bharat, Shresth Bharat', Bharatiya Janata Party Election Manifesto, 2014.

Bharatiya Janata Party. 'Sankalpit Bharat, Sashakt Bharat', Bharatiya Janata Party Sankalp Patra, Lok Sabha, 2019.

Discussion on the Motion Regarding the Bengal Situation, 7 August 1950, Parliament, Second Session of the Parliament of India, *Parliamentary Debates,* Vol. 4, 1950.

Divya Goyal. 'Sikhs and Hindus of Afghanistan — how many remain, why they want to leave', *The Indian Express*, 28 July 2020, https://indianexpress.com/article/explained/sikhs-and-hindus-of-afghanistan-how-many-remain-why-they-want-to-leave-6524825/

Farhanaz Ispahani. '*Pakistan's Descent into Religious Intolerance*', Commentary, 1 March. Washington DC: Hudson Institute, 2017.

Farhanaz Ispahani. *Purifying the Land of the Pure: Pakistan's Religious Minorities*. New Delhi: Harper Collins, 2015.

Himanshu Mishra. 'PM Modi chairs high-level meet on Afghan situation, directs officials to ensure safe evacuation of all Indians', *India Today*, 18 August 2021, https://www.indiatoday.in/india/story/pm-modi-high-level-meet-afghan-situation-directs-officials-ensure-safe-evacuation-indians-1842070-2021-08-17

Indrajit Kundu. 'Coronavirus panic to divert attention from Delhi riots: Mamata Banerjee slams Modi government', 4 March 2020, https://www.indiatoday.in/india/story/coronavirus-delhi-riots-mamata-banerjee-1652324-2020-03-04

Jayanta Kumar Ray. *Democracy and Nationalism on Trial: A Study of East Pakistan*. Simla: Indian Institute of Advanced Study, 1968.

Md Kamrul Hasan. 'No Hindus will be left after 30 years', *Dhaka Tribune*, 20 November 2016, https://www.dhakatribune.com/bangladesh/10113/%E2%80%98no-hindus-will-be-left-after-30-years

PM Modi's blog. 'PM Modi's Bond with the Sikh Community', https://www.narendramodi.in/prime-minister-narendra-modis-bond-with-the-sikh-community-576651

Press Release, Pallone Expresses Concern Regarding Persecution of Hindus in Bangladesh', 18 May 2004, https://pallone.house.gov/press-release/pallone-expresses-concern-regarding-persecution-hindus-bangledesh.

PTI. 'Go for UN monitored referendum on CAA, NRC: Mamata Banerjee's Challenge to Centre', *Times of India*, 19 December 2019, https://timesofindia.indiatimes.com/india/go-for-un-monitored-referendum-on-caa-nrc-mamata-banerjees-challenge-to-centre/articleshow/72887680.cms

Sachi G. Dastidar. *Bengal's Hindu Holocaust: The Partition of India and Its Aftermath*. Gurugram: Garuda Prakashan, 2021.

Salam Azad. *Hindu Sampraday Keno Deshatyag Korchhe*. Kolkata: Swatantra Prakashani, 1405 (Bengali era).

Samson Salamat's testimony to the UN Commission on Human Rights Working Group on Minorities 10th Session, 1–5 March 2004.

Senge Hasnan Sering. 'Survival of Democracy and Minorities in Pakistan Rests with Separating Religion from Politics', *Firstpost*, https://www.

firstpost.com/world/survival-of-democracy-and-minorities-in-pakistan-rests-with-separating-religious-from-politics-8457531.html

Simrin Sirur. 'Bangladeshi Would Rather Swim to Italy than Come to India, Says Outgoing Envoy', 20 November 2019, https://theprint.in/diplomacy/bangladeshis-would-rather-swim-to-italy-than-come-to-india-says-outgoing-envoy/323985/

Suhrid Shankar Chattopadhyay. 'West Bengal Assembly Passes Anti-CAA Resolution', *Frontline*, 22 February 2020.

Tilak Devasher. 'In Pak, Wither Minorities', *The Tribune*, 1 June 2020.

Tilak Devasher. 'Making Minorities Insecure', *The Tribune*, 10 February 2020.

Tilak Devasher. 'Pak's Ideological Insecurity', *The Tribune*, 10 August 2020.

Tilak Devasher. 'Pakistan and the Citizenship Amendment Act', https://www.aninews.in/news/world/asia/pakistan-and-the-citizenship-amendment-act20191220123521/

Chapter 6: Communist Perfidy on CAA

A.J. Kamra. *The Prolonged Partition and Its Programs: Testimonies on Violence against Hindus in East Bengal 1946–64*. New Delhi: Voice of India, 2000.

Arun Shourie. *The Only Fatherland: Communists, Quit India and the Soviet Union* (1991). New Delhi: Harper Collins, 2014.

Deep Halder. *Blood Island: An Oral History of the Marichjhapi Massacre*. New Delhi: Harper Collins, 2019.

Nitish Sengupta. *Bengal Divided: The Unmaking of a Nation – 1905–1971*. New Delhi: Penguin, 2007.

Prafulla Chakrabarti. *The Marginal Men: The Refugees and the Left Political Syndrome in West Bengal*. Kolkata: Naya Udyog, 1999.

Rammanohar Lohia. *Guilty Men of India's Partition*, 4th ed. New Delhi: B.R. Publishing Corporation, 2000 (1960).

Ross Mallick. 'Refugee Resettlement in Forest Reserves: West Bengal Policy Reversal and the Marichjhapi Massacre'. *The Journal of Asian Studies*, 58 (1) (Feb. 1999).

Ross Mallick. *Development Policy of a Communist Government*. New Delhi: Cambridge University Press, 1993.

Sukha Ranjan Sengupta. *Jyoti Basu ke Chinechilen Syama Prasad.* Kolkata: Gangchil, 2012.

Sunanda Sanyal and Soumya Basu. *The Sickle and the Crescent: Communists, Muslim League and India's Partition.* Kolkata: Frontpage Publications, 2011.

White Paper on Citizenship Amendment Act, New Delhi: Dr Syama Prasad Mookerjee Research Foundation, 2020.

Chapter 7: Keeping the Promise: Struggle for Refugees and Citizenship over the Decades—RSS, Jana Sangh, BJP

Bharatiya Jana Sangh (1952-1980): Party Document—Policies and Manifestoes, vol. 1. New Delhi: Bharatiya Janata Party, 2005.

Bharatiya Jana Sangh: Party Document—Defence and External Affairs, vol. 3, 2005.

Bharatiya Jana Sangh: Party Document—Education and Party Affairs, vol. 5, 2005.

Bharatiya Jana Sangh: Party Document—Internal Affairs, vol. 4, 2005.

C.P. Bhishikar. *Shri Guruji: Pioneer of a New Era,* translated by Sudhakar Raje. Bangalore: Sahitya Sindhu Prakashana, 1999.

Complete Works of Deendayal Upadhyaya (CWDDU), vols 2, 4, 11, 12. New Delhi: Prabhat Prakashan & Research & Development Foundation for Integral Humanism, 2019.

N.M. Ghatate, ed. *Atal Bihari Vajpayee: Four Decades in Parliament,* Foreign Affairs, vol. 3. New Delhi: Shipra Publications, 1996.

Postscript

Richard Pilkington. *The West and the Birth of Bangladesh: Foreign Policy in the Face of Mass Atrocity.* 2021.

Naba Kumar Adak. *Syama Prasad Mookerjee: A Study in Bengal Politics (1929-1953).* 2013.

V.S. Gupta. 'Refugee Problem'. *Organiser,* 11 September 1947.

Index

About the Author

Dr Anirban Ganguly is the chairman of Dr Syama Prasad Mookerjee Research Foundation, New Delhi. He is a member of BJP's National Executive Committee. Besides being a political activist, he has extensively worked in the areas of public policy and political research. He has a PhD from Jadavpur University, Kolkata, on the national education movement in India and Sri Aurobindo's education philosophy. Dr Ganguly is also a scholar of civilisation, history, politics, and culture and has written and continues to write on these subjects. He was a member of the Central Advisory Board of Education (CABE); Indian National Commission for Cooperation with UNESCO (INCCU); Governing Board of Auroville Foundation; and Visva-Bharati Samsad (Court), Santiniketan. He writes newspaper columns and has authored, co-authored, and edited several books including *Subhas Chandra O Syama Prasad: Tulanamulok Chintan Aloke* (2024), *Modi: Energising a Green Future* (2023), *The Master: Sri Aurobindo and the Quest for National Education* (2023), *K.R. Malkani and the Motherland* (2022), *Modi 2.0: A Resolve to Secure India* (2021), *Dattopant Thengadi: The Activist Parliamentarian* (2020), *Amit Shah and the March of BJP* (2019), *Making of*

New India: Transformation under Modi Government (2018), *Syama Prasad Mookerjee: His Vision of Education* (2017), *The Modi Doctrine: New Paradigms in India's Foreign Policy* (2016), *Redefining Governance: Essays on One year of Narendra Modi Government* (2015), *Swami Vivekananda, Buddha and Buddhism* (2014), *Debating Culture* (2013), and *Education: Philosophy and Practice* (2011).